THE ARAB REVOLT AND THE IMPERIALIST COUNTERATTACK

THE ARAB REVOLT AND THE IMPERIALIST COUNTERATTACK

SECOND EDITION

JAMES PETRAS

CLARITY PRESS, INC.

© 2012 James Petras

ISBN: 0-98527-10-0-0
      978-0-98527-10-0-8

First Edition 2011, Clear Day Books.

In-house editor: Diana G. Collier
Cover: R. Jordan P. Santos
Images (top) The B-2 Spirit bomber. (U.S. Air Force photo/Staff Sgt.
        Bennie J. Davis III)
        (bottom) The March of Anger, Friday, Cairo, Feb. 4, 2011
        by Amr Farouq Mohammed Ahmed

Library of Congress Cataloging-in-Publication Data

Petras, James F., 1937-
   The Arab revolt and the imperialist counterattack / by James Petras. -- 2nd ed.
      p. cm.
   ISBN 978-0-9852710-0-8 -- ISBN 0-9852710-0-0
   1. United States--Foreign relations--Arab countries. 2. Arab countries--Foreign
relations--United States. 3. Arab countries--Politics and government--21st
century. 4. United States--Foreign relations--Egypt. 5. Egypt--Foreign relations-
-United States. 6. Egypt--Politics and government--21st century. 7. United
States--Foreign relations--Libya. 8. Libya--Foreign relations--United States. 9.
Libya--Politics and government--21st century. I. Title.

   DS63.2.U5P49 2012
   327.730174927--dc23

2011052114

Clarity Press, Inc.
Ste. 469, 3277 Roswell Rd. NE
Atlanta, GA. 30305 , USA
http://www.claritypress.com

To the Arab revolutionaries struggling
against Western imperialism
and collaborater dictatorships

TABLE OF CONTENTS

Introduction / 11

Chapter 1`
Washington Faces the Arab Revolts:
Sacrificing Dictators to Save the State / 15

Chapter 2
Egypt's Social Movements, The CIA and Mossad / 23

Chapter 3
Roots of the Arab Revolts and
Premature Celebrations / 29

Chapter 4
The Euro-US War on Libya
Official Lies and Misconceptions of Critics / 41

Chapter 5
Libya and Obama's Defense of the 'Rebel Uprising' / 55

Chapter 6
Contextualizing the 'Arab Spring':
Networks of Empire and Realignments of World Power / 60

Chapter 7
NATO's War Crimes in Libya:
Who Grieves for the Fallen Heroes? / 74

Chapter 8
The Assassination of Osama Bin Laden
Its Uses and Abuses / 87

Chapter 9
The Assassination of Anwar Al-Awlaki by Fiat / 93

Chapter 9
The Obama Doctrine: Making a Virtue of Necessity / 99

Chapter 10
What Future for the Washington / "Moderate Islam"
Alliance? / 111

APPENDIX
Indicators of Social Well Being in Pre-Invasion Libya / 123

INDEX / 128

INTRODUCTION

The US bombing of Libya in support of rebel clients in the spring of 2011 is part and parcel of a sustained policy of military intervention in Africa since at least the mid 1950s. According to a US Congressional Research Service Study[1] published in November 2010, Washington has dispatched anywhere between hundreds and several thousand combat troops, dozens of fighter planes and warships to buttress client dictatorships or to unseat adversarial regimes in dozens of countries, almost on a yearly basis. The record shows the US armed forces intervened 46 times prior to the current Libyan war.[2] The countries suffering one or more US military interventions include the Congo, Zaire, Libya, Chad, Sierra Leone, Somalia, Ruanda, Liberia, Central African Republic, Gabon, Guinea-Bissau, Kenya, Tanzania, Sudan, Ivory Coast, Ethiopia, Djibouti and Eritrea. The only progressive intervention was in Egypt under Eisenhower who forced the Israeli-French-English forces to withdraw from the Suez in 1956.

Between the mid 1950s to the end of the 1970s, only 4 overt military operations were recorded, though *large scale proxy and clandestine military operations* were pervasive. Under Reagan-Bush Sr. (1980-1991) military intervention accelerated, rising to 8, *not counting the large scale clandestine 'special forces' and proxy wars in Southern Africa*. Under the Clinton regime, US militarized imperialism in Africa took off. Between 1992 and 2000, 17 armed incursions took place, including a large scale invasion of Somalia and military backing for the Ruanda genocidal regime.[3] Clinton intervened in Liberia, Gabon, Congo and Sierra Leone to prop up a longstanding stooge regime. He bombed the Sudan and dispatched military personnel to Kenya and Ethiopia to back proxy clients assaulting Somalia. Under Bush Jr., 15 US military interventions took place, mainly in Central and East Africa. The Obama regime's invasion and bombing of Libya is thus a continuation of a longstanding imperial practice designed to enhance US power via the installation of client regimes, the establishment of military bases and the training and indoctrination of African mercenary forces. There is no question that there is a rising tide of imperial militarism in the US over the past several decades.

Most of the US' African empire is disproportionally built on military links to client military chiefs. The Pentagon has military ties with 53 African countries (including Libya prior to the current attack). Washington's efforts to militarize Africa and turn its armies into proxy mercenaries to serve in putting down anti-imperial revolts and regimes were accelerated after 9/11. The Bush Administration announced in 2002 that Africa was a "strategic priority in fighting terrorism".[4] Henceforth, US imperial strategists, with the backing of liberal and neoconservative Congress-people, moved to centralize and coordinate a military policy on a continent-wide basis, forming the African Command (AFRICOM). The latter organizes African armies, euphemistically called "co-operative partnerships," to conduct neo-colonial wars based on bilateral agreements (Uganda, Burundi, etc.) as well as 'multilateral' links with the Organization of African Unity.[5]

AFRICOM, despite its assigned role as a vehicle for spreading imperial influence, has been more successful in *destroying countries* than in gaining resources and power bases. The war against Somalia, displacing and killing millions and costing hundreds of millions of dollars, enters its twentieth year, with no victory in sight. Apart from the longest standing US neo-colony, Liberia, there has been no country willing to allow AFRICOM to set up headquarters.

Most significantly AFRICOM was unprepared for the overthrow of key client regimes in Tunisia and Egypt— important "partners" in patrolling the North African Mediterranean, the Arabian coast and the Red Sea. Despite Libya's collaboration with AFRICOM, especially in "anti-terrorist" intelligence operations, Washington mistakenly believed that an easy victory by its "rebel" clients might lead to a more docile regime, offering more in the way of a military base, headquarters and a cheap source of oil. Today the US depends as much on African petroleum as on its suppliers in the Middle East.

The continent-wide presence of AFRICOM has been matched by its incapacity to convert "partnerships" into effective proxy conquerors. The attempt to foster "civil-military" programs has failed to secure any popular base for corrupt collaborator regimes, valued for their willingness to provide imperial cannon fodder.

The continuing North African uprising has overthrown the public face of the imperial backed dictatorships in the Middle East. As the popular Arab revolt spreads to the Gulf and deepens its demands to include socio-economic as well as political demands, the Empire struck back. AFRICOM backed the assault on Libya, the crackdown on the prodemocracy movement by the ruling military junta in Egypt and looks to its autocratic "partners" in the Gulf and the Arabian Peninsula to drown the civil society movements in a blood bath.

These essays chronicle the growing militarization of US policy in North Africa and the Gulf and the historic confrontation between the Arab democratic revolution and the imperial backed satraps; between Libyans fighting for their independence and the Euro-American naval and air forces ravaging the country on behalf of their inept local clients.

ENDNOTES

1   Lauren Ploch, Africa Command: US strategic Interests and the Role of the Military in Africa (Congressional Research Service <CRS> Nov. 16, 2010.

2   Richard Grimmett, Instances of Use of United States Armed Forces Abroad 1798-2009 (CRS 2010).

3   Edward Herman "Gilbert Achar's Defense of Humanitarian Intervention" (ZNET April 8, 2011)

4   The White House, National Security Strategy of the United States (September 2002).

5   Lauren Ploch, op. cit., esp. pp.19-25.

WASHINGTON FACES THE ARAB REVOLTS

SACRIFICING DICTATORS TO SAVE THE STATE

Introduction

To understand the Obama regime's policy toward Egypt, the Mubarak dictatorship and the popular uprising, it is essential to locate it in an historical context. The essential point is that Washington, after several decades of being deeply embedded in the state structures of the Arab dictatorships, from Tunisia through Morocco, Egypt, Yemen, Lebanon, Saudi Arabia and the Palestinian Authority, is attempting to re-orient its policies to incorporate and/or graft liberal-electoral politicians onto the existing power configurations.

While most commentators and journalists spill tons of ink about the "dilemmas" of US power, the novelty of the Egyptian events and Washington's day to day policy pronouncements, there are ample historical precedents which are essential to understand the strategic direction of Obama's policies.

Historical Background

US foreign policy has a long history of installing, financing, arming and backing dictatorial regimes which back its imperial policies and interests as long as they retain control over their people.

In the past, Republican and Democratic presidents worked closely for over 30 years with the Trujillo dictatorship in the Dominican Republic; installed the autocratic Diem regime in pre-revolutionary Vietnam in the 1950's; collaborated with two generations of Somoza family terror regimes in Nicaragua; financed and promoted the military coup in Cuba in 1952, Brazil in 1964, Chile in 1973, and in Argentina in 1976 and the subsequent repressive regimes. When popular upheavals challenged these US backed dictatorships, and a social as well as political revolution appeared likely to succeed, Washington responded with a three track policy: *publically* criticizing the human rights violations and advocating democratic reforms; *privately* signaling continued support to the ruler; and thirdly, seeking an elite alternative which could substitute for the incumbent *and* preserve the state apparatus, the economic system and support US strategic imperial interests.

For the US there are no strategic relationships only permanent imperial interests, namely preservation of the client *state*. The dictatorships assume that their relationships with Washington are strategic : hence the shock and dismay when they are sacrificed personally in order to save the state apparatus. Fearing revolution, Washington has had reluctant client despots, unwilling to move on, assassinated (Trujillo and Diem). Some are provided sanctuaries abroad (Somoza, Batista),others are pressured into power-sharing (Pinochet) or appointed as visiting scholars to Harvard, Georgetown or some other "prestigious" academic posting.

The Washington calculus on when to reshuffle the regime is based on an estimate of the capacity of the dictator to weather the political uprising, the strength and loyalty of the armed forces and the availability of a pliable replacement. The risk of waiting too long, of sticking with the dictator, is that the uprising radicalizes: the ensuing change sweeps away both the regime *and* the state apparatus, turning a political uprising into a social revolution. Just such a 'miscalculation' occurred in 1959 in the run-up to the Cuban revolution, when Washington stood by Batista and was not able to present a viable pro US alternative coalition that was still linked to the old state apparatus. A similar miscalculation occurred in Nicaragua, when President Carter, while criticizing Somoza, stayed the course, and stood passively by as the regime was overthrown and the revolutionary forces destroyed the US and Israeli-trained military, secret police and intelligence apparatus, and went on to nationalize US property and develop an independent foreign policy.

Washington moved with greater initiative in Latin America in the 1980's. It promoted negotiated electoral transitions which replaced dictators with pliable neoliberal electoral politicians, who pledged to preserve the existing state apparatus, defend the privileged foreign and domestic elites and back US regional and international policies.

Past Lessons and Present Policies

Obama was extremely hesitant to oust Mubarak for several reasons, even as the movement grew in number and anti-Washington sentiment deepens. The White House has many clients around the world – including Honduras, Mexico, Indonesia, Jordan and Algeria – who believe they have a strategic relationship with Washington and would lose confidence in their future if Mubarak were dumped.

Secondly, the highly influential leading pro-Israel organizations in the US (AIPAC, the Presidents of the Major American Jewish Organizations) and their army of scribes mobilized congressional leaders to pressure the White House to continue backing Mubarak, as Israel was the prime beneficiary of a dictator who was at the throat of the Egyptians (and Palestinians) and at the feet of the Jewish state.

As a result, the Obama regime moved slowly, under fear

and pressure of the growing Egyptian popular movement. It searched for an alternative political formula that removed Mubarak, retained and strengthened the political power of the state apparatus, and incorporated a civilian electoral alternative as a means of demobilizing and de-radicalizing the vast popular movement.

The major obstacle to ousting Mubarak was that a major sector of the state apparatus, especially the 325,000 Central Security Forces and the 60,000 member National Guard, were directly under the Interior Ministry and Mubarak. Secondly, top generals in the Army (468,500 members) have buttressed Mubarak for 30 years and have been enriched by their control over very lucrative companies in a wide range of fields. They would not support any civilian 'coalition' that called into question their economic privileges and power to set the political parameters of any electoral system. The supreme commander of the Egyptian military is a longtime client of the US and a willing collaborator with Israel.

Obama is resolutely in favor of collaborating with and ensuring the preservation of these coercive bodies. But he also needed to convince them to replace Mubarak and allow for a new regime which can defuse the mass movement which is increasingly opposed to US hegemony and Egyptian subservience to Israel. Obama did everything necessary to retain the cohesion of the state and avoid any splits which might lead to a mass movement/soldier alliance which could convert the uprising into a revolution.

Washington opened talks with the most conservative liberal and clerical sectors of the anti-Mubarak movement. At first it tried to convince them to *negotiate* with Mubarak – a dead end position which was rejected by all sectors of the opposition, top and bottom. Then Obama tried to sell a phony "promise" from Mubarak that he would not run in the elections, nine months later.

The movement and its leaders rejected that proposal also. So Obama raised the rhetoric for 'immediate changes' but without any substantive measures backing it up. To convince Obama of his continued power base, Mubarak sent his formidable thug-lumpen secret police to violently seize the streets from the movement. In the ensuing test of strength, the Army stood by; the assault raised the ante of a civil war, with radical consequences. Washington and the EU pressured the Mubarak regime to back off. But the image of a pro-democracy military was tarnished, as killings and injuries multiplied in the thousands.

As the pressure of the movement intensified, Obama was cross pressured by the pro-Mubarak Israel Lobby and its Congressional entourage on the one hand, and on the other by knowledgeable advisors who called on him to follow past practices and move decisively to sacrifice the regime to save the state while the liberal-clerical electoral option is still on the table.

But Obama hesitated and like a wary crustacean, he moved sideways and backwards, believing his own grandiloquent rhetoric is a substitute for action ... hoping that sooner or later, the uprising would end with Mubarakism without Mubarak: a regime able to demobilize the popular movements and willing to promote elections which would result in elected officials following the general line of their predecessor.

Nevertheless, there are many uncertainties in a political reshuffle: a democratic citizenry, over 80% unfavorable to Washington, will possess the experience of struggle and the freedom to call for a realignment of policy, especially to cease being a policeman enforcing the Israeli blockage of Gaza, and providing support for US puppets in North Africa, Lebanon, Yemen, Jordan and Saudi Arabia. Secondly free elections could open debate and increase pressure for greater social spending; the expropriation of the seventy billion dollar empire of the Mubarak clan and the crony capitalists who pillage the economy. The masses could demand a reallocation of public expenditure from the overblown coercive apparatus to productive, job generating employment. The limited political opening has led to a second round, in which new social and political conflicts divide the post-Mubarak forces. The key issue is whether neoliberalism itself will be challenged. The anti-dictatorial moment is only the first phase of a prolonged struggle toward definitive emancipation not only in Egypt but throughout the Arab world. The outcome depends on the degree to which the masses develop their own independent organization and leaders. If a social democratic alternative were to come into effective being, it would surely take up this challenge.

Problems in "Sacrificing" the Mubarak Regime

By the end of the first 18 days of the Egyptian uprising, with demonstrators numbering in the millions and the *exposure* of the complicity and/or immobility of the Obama regime radicalizing the crowd, it was clear that Washington could not "engineer" the change of regime by itself, it required the direct intervention of the military.

Mubarak refused to resign and Obama could not move him because, unlike other evictions of dictators, Congress and powerful financial backers of the President strongly objected. On February 9-10, 2011, the US Congressional Committee on Foreign Affairs held a hearing on Egypt. The committee was chaired by Republican Ileana Ros-Lehtinen, a Zionist hardliner and unconditional backer of Israeli policy supporting Mubarak. The ranking minority member is Democratic ultra-Zionist, Howard Berman. The committee's "expert witnesses" included four pro-Israel hardliners, no pro-democracy advocates. Lobbyists Robert Satloff and Elliott Abrams are virulent enemies of any critic of Israel and strong advocates of the Iraq war. Abrams served in the Bush White House. Other "experts" included James Steinberg from the State Department and Lorne Cramer, both strong supporters of Israeli militarism ("security") in the Middle East. As was predictable, the Committee "findings" echoed Israel's line backing Mubarak's continued tenure in office and warned of the "Islamic dangers" if a democratic revolution succeeded. The entire 80,000 member American Israel Political Action Committee responded to Netanyahu's call, exercising maximum pressure in support of Vice President Suleiman, the slavishly subservient former torture chief of the dictator and of the high command of the military led by Mubarak's Defense Minister.

Unlike previous uprisings where the President had a free hand (little internal Congressional opposition) in sacrificing a dictator to save the state, in the case of Egypt, the powerful Jewish-Zionist lobby undercut the process. Obama was led to promote Mubarak's handpicked protégé, Omar Suleiman as a legitimate interlocutor, even as he was rejected by the multitude of pro-democracy demonstrators. The United Nations Secretary General Ban Ki-Moon further disgraced his office by following Obama's lead and calling for dialogue and negotiations with Mubarak's puppet, Suleiman.

With Mubarak openly threatening an Indonesian style mass massacre if the Egyptian citizenry did not disband, and Suleiman openly posing the choice as between Mubarak or a military coup, and the working class and trade unions calling for a general strike, a civil war was averted by the military takeover with backing from liberal democratic politicians.

Imperial linkages to a militarist state (Israel) are a distinct liability, in flexibly choosing liberal alternatives to safeguard strategic geo-political interests i.e. the Suez Canal, stable pro-western civilian regimes (like Turkey) and leverage within Egyptian civil society.

Because the continuance of Mubarak in power hastened the radicalization of the uprising, as evidenced by the entry of the trade unions and working class who supported an indefinite general strike, the military intervened. The scarcity of food and skyrocketing prices increased the social desperation among the multitude of poor who ring the central cities. Obama, the UN and the European Union's double discourse of democratic rhetoric and backing of Mubarak stooge Suleiman heightened anti-imperialist feelings. The initial student-led demonstrations focused on anti-dictatorial demands but detonated an increasingly social and anti-imperialist mass movement moving beyond the objectives of the middle class.

The uprising entered a critical phase, a time of living dangerously. The military decided to ease out the dictatorship, to avoid a collapse under pressure from the mass movement which might threaten its property, wealth and power. After Mubarak, there was a scramble for power between all the forces in opposition. They included former US and Israeli collaborators, democrats, socialists, liberals, Islamists and local leaders of impoverished excluded people seeking to promote a constitutional order based on civil supremacy, political independence and social democracy. Phase two of the struggle began with the fall of Mubarak.

EGYPT'S SOCIAL MOVEMENTS, THE CIA AND MOSSAD

The Limits of Social Movements

The mass movements which forced the removal of Mubarak reveal both the strength and weaknesses of spontaneous uprisings. On the one hand, the social movements demonstrated their capacity to mobilize hundreds of thousands, if not millions, in a successful sustained struggle culminating in the overthrow of the dictator in a way that pre-existent opposition parties and personalities were unable or unwilling to do.

On the other hand, lacking any national political leadership, the movements were not able to take political power and realize their demands. This allowed the Mubarak military high command to seize power and define the "post-Mubarak" process, ensuring the continuation of Egypt's subordination to the US, and the protection of the illicit wealth of the Mubarak clan ($70 billion), as well as the military elite's numerous corporations and the protection of the upper class. The millions mobilized by the social movements to overthrow the dictatorship were effectively excluded by the new self-styled "revolutionary" military junta in defining the political institutions and policies, let along the socio-economic reforms needed to address their basic needs of the population (40% live on less than $2

USD a day, youth unemployment runs over 30%). Egypt, as in the case of the student and popular social movements against the dictatorships of South Korea, Taiwan, Philippines and Indonesia, demonstrates that the lack of a national political organization allows neoliberal and conservative "opposition" personalities and parties to replace the regime. They proceed to set up an electoral regime which continues to serve imperial interests and to depend on and defend the existing state apparatus. In some cases they replace old crony capitalists with new ones. It is no accident that the mass media praise the 'spontaneous' nature of the struggles (not the socio-economic demands) and put a favorable spin on the role of the military (slighting its 30 years as a bulwark of the dictatorship). The masses are praised for their "heroism", the youth for their "idealism", but are *never proposed* as central political actors in the new regime. Once the dictatorship fell, the military and the opposition electoralists "celebrated" the success of the revolution and moved swiftly to demobilize and dismantle the spontaneous movement, in order to make way for negotiations between the liberal electoral politicians, Washington and the ruling military elite.

While the White House may tolerate or even promote social movements in ousting ("sacrificing") dictatorships, it has every intention of preserving the state. In the case of Egypt the main strategic ally of US imperialism was not Mubarak, it is the military, with whom Washington was in constant collaboration before, during and after the ouster of Mubarak, ensuring that the "transition" to democracy (sic) guarantees the continued subordination of Egypt to US and Israeli Middle East policy and interests.

The Revolt of the People: The Failures of the CIA and Mossad

The Arab revolt demonstrates once again several strategic failures in the much vaunted secret police, special forces and intelligence agencies of the US and Israeli state apparatus, none of which anticipated, let alone intervened, to preclude successful mobilization and influence their government's policy toward the client rulers under attack.

The image which most writers, academics and journalists project of the invincibility of the Israeli Mossad and of the omnipotent CIA have been severely tested by their admitted failure to recognize the scope, depth and intensity of the multi-million member movement to oust the Mubarak dictatorship. The Mossad, pride and joy of Hollywood producers, presented as a 'model of efficiency' by their organized Zionist colleagues, were not able to detect the growth of a mass movement in a country right next door. Israeli Prime Minister Netanyahu was shocked (and dismayed) by the precarious situation of Mubarak and the collapse of his most prominent Arab client – left unprepared because of Mossad's faulty intelligence. Likewise, Washington was totally unprepared for the forthcoming massive popular uprisings and emerging movements by its 27 US intelligence agencies and the Pentagon, with their hundreds of thousands of paid operatives and multi-billion dollar budgets.

Several theoretical observations are in order. The notion that highly repressive rulers receiving billions of dollars of US military aid and with close to a million police, military and paramilitary forces are the best guarantors of imperial hegemony has been demonstrated to be false. The assumption that large scale, long term links with such dictatorial rulers, safeguards US imperial interests has been disproved.

Israeli arrogance and presumption of Jewish organizational, strategic and political superiority over "the Arabs" has been severely deflated. The Israeli state, its experts, undercover operatives and Ivy League academics were blind to the unfolding realities, ignorant of the depth of disaffection and impotent to prevent the mass opposition to their most valued client. Israel's publicists in the US, who scarcely resist the opportunity to promote the "brilliance" of Israel's security forces, whether it's assassinating an Arab leader in Lebanon or Dubai, or bombing a military facility in Syria, were temporarily speechless.

The fall of Mubarak and the *possible* emergence of an independent and democratic government would mean that Israel could lose its major 'cop on the beat'. A democratic Egyptian public with the bit in its teeth will not cooperate with Israel in maintaining the blockade of Gaza – starving Palestinians to break their will to resist. Israel will not be able to count on a democratic government to back its violent land seizures in the West Bank and its stooge Palestinian regime. Nor can the US count on a democratic Egypt to back its intrigues in Lebanon, its wars in Iraq and Afghanistan, or its sanctions against Iran. Moreover, the Egyptian uprising has served as an example for popular movements against other US client dictatorships in Jordan, Yemen and Saudi Arabia. For all these reasons, Washington only backed the military takeover in order to shape a political transition according to its liking and imperial interests.

The weakening of the principal pillar of US imperial and Israeli colonial power in North Africa and the Middle East reveals the essential role of imperial collaborator regimes. The dictatorial character of these regimes is a direct result of the role they play in upholding imperial interests. And the major military aid packages which corrupt and enrich the ruling elites are the rewards for being willing collaborators of imperial and colonial states. Given the strategic importance of the Egyptian dictatorship, how do we explain the failure of the US and Israeli intelligence agencies to anticipate the uprisings?

Both the CIA and the Mossad worked *closely* with the Egyptian intelligence agencies and relied on them for their information, confiding in their self-serving reports that "everything was under control": the opposition parties were weak, decimated by repression ad infiltration, their militants languishing in jail, or suffering fatal "heart attacks" because of harsh "interrogation techniques". The elections were rigged to elect US and Israeli clients – no democratic surprises in the immediate or medium term horizon.

Egyptian intelligence agencies are trained and financed by Israeli and US operatives and are amenable to pursuing their masters will. They were so compliant in turning in reports which pleased their mentors, that they ignored any accounts of growing popular unrest or of internet agitation. The CIA and Mossad were so *embedded* in Mubarak's vast security apparatus that they were incapable of securing any other information from the grassroots, decentralized, burgeoning movements which were *independent* of the "controlled" traditional electoral opposition.

When the extra-parliamentary mass movements burst forward, the Mossad and the CIA counted on the Mubarak state apparatus to take control via the typical carrot and stick operation: transient token concessions while calling out the army, police and death squads. As the movement grew from tens of thousands to hundreds of thousands, to millions, the Mossad and leading US Congressional backers of Israel urged Mubarak to "hold on". The CIA was reduced to presenting the White House with political profiles of reliable military officials and pliable "transitional" political personages willing to follow in Mubarak's footsteps. Once again the CIA and Mossad demonstrated their dependence on the Mubarak apparatus for intelligence on who might be a "viable" (pro-US/Israel) alternative, ignoring the elementary demands of the masses. The attempt to co-opt the old guard electoralist Muslim Brotherhood via negotiations with Vice-President Suleiman failed, in part because the Brotherhood was not in control of the movement and because Israel and their US backers objected. Moreover, the youth wing of the Brotherhood pressured them to withdraw from the negotiations.

The intelligence failure complicated Washington and Tel Aviv's efforts to sacrifice the dictatorial regime to save the state: the CIA ad MOSSAD did not develop ties to any of the new emerging leaders. The Israelis could not find any 'new face' with a popular following willing to serve as a crass collaborator with colonial oppression. The CIA had been entirely engaged in using the Egyptian secret police for torturing terror suspects ("exceptional rendition") and in policing neighboring Arab countries. As a result both Washington and Israel looked to and promoted the military takeover to preempt further radicalization.

A few writers claim that the National Endowment for Democracy (NED) was behind the uprising because they may have funded some activists prior to the uprising. Be that as it may, what transpired in actuality was that the mass revolt and its demands went far beyond the kind of docile "alternatives" that NED typically prepares for "managed transitions". That the actual revolt did not reflect American intentions is evident in the struggles and see-sawing of Obama officials as to whether the US would support it or not.

Ultimately the failure of the CIA and MOSSAD to detect and prevent the rise of the popular democratic movement reveals the precarious bases of imperial and colonial power. Over the long run it is not arms, billions of dollars, secret police and torture chambers that decide history. Democratic revolutions occur when the vast majority of a people arise and say "enough", take the streets, paralyze the economy, dismantle the authoritarian state and demand freedom and democratic institutions without imperial tutelage and colonial subservience.

ROOTS OF THE ARAB REVOLTS AND PREMATURE CELEBRATIONS

Introduction

Most accounts of the Arab revolts from Egypt, Tunisia, Libya, Morocco, Yemen, Jordan, Bahrain, Iraq and elsewhere have focused on the most immediate causes: political dictatorships, unemployment, repression and the wounding and killing of protestors. They have given most attention to the "middle class", young, educated activists, their communication via the internet,[1] and, in the case of Israel and its Zionists conspiracy theorists, "the hidden hand" of Islamic extremists.[2]

What is lacking is any attempt to provide a framework for the revolt which takes account of the *large scale*, *long* and *medium term* socio-economic structures as well as the immediate 'detonators' of political action. The scope and depth of the popular uprisings, as well as the diverse political and social forces which have entered into the conflicts, preclude any explanations which look at one dimension of the struggles.

The best approach involves a 'funnel framework' in which, at the wide end (the long-term, large-scale structures), stands the nature of the economic, class and political system; the middle-term is defined by the dynamic cumulative effects of these structures on changes in political, social and economic relations; the short-term causes, which precipitate the socio-political-psychological responses, or social consciousness leading to political action.

The Nature of the Arab Economies

With the exception of Jordan, most of the Arab economies where the revolts are taking place are based on 'rents' from oil, gas, minerals and tourism, which provide most of the export earnings and state revenues.[3] These economic sectors are, in effect, *export enclaves* employing a tiny fraction of the labor force and define a highly specialized economy.[4] These export sectors do not have links to a diversified productive domestic economy: oil is exported and finished manufactured goods as well as financial and high tech services are all imported and controlled by foreign multinationals and ex-pats linked to the ruling class.[5] Tourism reinforces 'rental' income, as the sector which provides 'foreign exchange' and tax revenues to the class–clan state. The latter relies on state-subsidized foreign capital and local politically connected 'real estate' developers for investment and imported foreign construction laborers.

Rent-based income may generate great *wealth*, especially as energy prices soar, but the funds accrue to a class of "rentiers" who have *no* vocation or inclination for deepening and extending the process of economic development and innovation. The rentiers "specialize" in financial speculation, overseas investments via private equity firms, extravagant consumption of high-end luxury goods and billion-dollar and billion-euro secret private accounts in overseas banks.

The rentier economy provides few jobs in modern productive activity; the *high end* is controlled by extended family-clan members and foreign financial corporations via ex-pat experts; technical and low-end employment is taken up by *contract* foreign labor, at income levels and working conditions below what the skilled local labor force is willing to accept.

The enclave rentier economy leads to a clan-based ruling class which 'confounds' public and private ownership: the actual state structure resembles that of absolutist monarchies, with the ruler and their extended families at the top and their client tribal/clan leaders, political entourage and technocrats in the middle.

These are "closed ruling classes". Entry is confined to select members of the clan or family dynasties and a small number of "entrepreneurial" individuals who might accumulate wealth servicing the ruling clan-class. The 'inner circle' lives off of rental income, secures payoffs from partnerships in real estate where they provide no skills, but only official permits, land grants, import licenses and tax holidays.

Beyond pillaging the public treasury, the ruling clan-class is required to promote 'free trade', i.e. importing cheap finished products, thus undermining any indigenous domestic start-ups in the 'productive' manufacturing, agricultural or technical sector.

As a result there is no entrepreneurial national capitalist or 'middle class'. What passes for a middle class are largely public sector *employees* (teachers, health professionals, functionaries, firemen, police officials, military officers) who depend on their salaries, which, in turn, depend on their subservience to absolutist power. They have no chance of advancing to the higher echelons or of opening economic opportunities for their educated offspring.

The concentration of economic, social and political power in a closed clan-class controlled system leads to an enormous concentration of wealth. Given the social *distance* between rulers and ruled, the wealth generated by high commodity prices produces a highly distorted image of per-capital "wealth"; adding billionaires and millionaires on top of a mass of low-income and underemployed youth provides a deceptively high average income.[6]

Rentier Rule: By Arms and Handouts

To compensate for these great disparities in society and to protect the position of the parasitical rentier ruling class, the latter are forced to pursue *alliances* with multi-billion dollar arms corporations, and seek military protection from the dominant (USA) imperial power. The rulers engage in "neo-colonization by invitation", offering land for military bases and airfields, ports for naval operations, and collude in financing proxy mercenaries against anti-imperial adversaries. They submit to Zionist hegemony in the region (despite occasional inconsequential criticisms).

In the middle term, rule by force is complemented by *paternalistic* handouts to the rural poor and tribal clans; food subsidies for the urban poor; and dead-end make-work employment for the educated unemployed.[7] Both costly arms purchases and paternalistic subsidies reflect the lack of any capacity for productive investments. Billions are spent on arms rather than diversifying the economy. Hundreds of millions are spent on one-shot paternalistic handouts, rather than long-term investments generating productive employment.

The 'glue' holding this system together is the combination of modern pillage of public wealth and natural energy resources and the use of traditional clan and neo-colonial recruits and mercenary contractors to control and repress the population. US modern armaments are at the service of anachronistic absolutist monarchies and dictatorships, based on the principles of 18th century dynastic rule.

The introduction and extension of the most up-to-date communication systems and ultra-modern architecture shopping centers cater to an elite strata of luxury consumers and provide a stark contrast to the vast majority of unemployed educated youth, excluded from the top and pressured from below by low-paid overseas contract workers.

Neoliberal Destabilization

While with regard to the oil kingdoms, it is correct to speak of rentier states lacking local entrepreneurship or development initiative, with regard to countries like Egypt, their backwardness is a result of both massive pillage of the public treasury and, a gamut of neoliberal policies enforced by the IMF, thus crippling the states' capacities to develop the forces of production. With regard to Egypt, one writer claims "[i]n addition to spreading poverty at an alarming rate, the so-called economic reforms recommended by the United States and the IMF have caused an unprecedented surge in unemployment and increased income inequality over the past three decades. According to official data, 2.4 million Egyptians are currently unemployed, but the real number could be more than 8 million, according to independent estimates."[8]

The rentier class-clans are pressured by the international financial institutions and local bankers to 'reform' their economies: 'open' the domestic market and public enterprises to foreign investors and reduce deficits resulting from the global crises by introducing neoliberal reforms.[9]

As a result of "economic reforms" food subsidies for the poor have been lowered or eliminated and state employment has been reduced, closing off one of the few opportunities for educated youth. Taxes on consumers and salaried/wage workers are increased while the real estate developers, financial speculators and importers receive tax exonerations. De-regulation has exacerbated massive corruption, not only among the rentier ruling class-clan, but also by their immediate business entourage.

The paternalistic 'bonds' tying the lower and middle class to the ruling class have been eroded by foreign-induced neoliberal "reforms", which combine 'modern' foreign exploitation with the existing "traditional" forms of domestic private pillage. The class-clan regimes no longer can rely on the clan, tribal, clerical and clientelistic loyalties to isolate urban trade unions, student, small business and low paid public sector movements.

There are two levels of client relations, internal and external: the internal one facilitates the client relationship between the imperial and the domestic leaderships. In the case of Egypt, the economy is further distorted by so-called aid – $200 million in economic aid from the US in 2009, contrasted with $1.3 billion in military aid annually – used largely to secure armaments with a view to strengthening the regime's domestic security. Beyond a primary objective of securing Egypt's peaceful relations with Israel, the "aid" actually facilitates the exaction of tribute:

> ... aid given to Egypt provides the United States with political, strategic, and sometimes economic benefits that far exceed the value of what Egypt has received. The conditions tied to U.S. aid ensure that much of the money returns to the United States, whether in the form of the imported American products, work contracts that go to American companies at less competitive prices than Egypt could have obtained had the bidding been open to international companies, or the salaries of USAID experts. Most important of all, this aid consolidated a gross imbalance in trade relations between Egypt and the U.S. During the 1983–2007

period, Egypt's total accumulated trade deficit with the United States was \$45.1 billion, according to the IMF Trade Statistics Trends Yearbook.[10]

The Street against the Palace

The 'immediate causes' of the Arab revolts are centered in the huge demographic-class contradictions of the clan-class ruled rentier economy. The ruling oligarchy rules over a mass of unemployed and underemployed young workers; between 50% to 65% of the population under 25 years of age.[11] The dynamic "modern" rentier economy does not incorporate the newly educated young into modern employment; it relegates them into the low-paid unprotected "informal economy" of the street as venders, transport and contract workers and in personal services. The ultra- modern oil, gas, real estate, tourism and shopping-mall sectors are dependent on the political and military support of backward traditional clerical, tribal and clan leaders, who are subsidized but never 'incorporated' into the sphere of modern production. The modern urban industrial working class with small, independent trade unions is banned. Middle class civic associations are either under state control or confined to petitioning the absolutist state.

The 'underdevelopment' of social organizations linked to social classes engaged in modern productive activity derives from the insignificance of the role of manufacturing in the economy itself. While indeed there were scatterings of strikes in Egypt during the revolt, the pivot of social and political action is the *street, conducted not by workers in industry—an insignificant sector of the economy—but rather by unemployed and underemployed part-time youth* engaged in the informal sector are found in the plazas, at kiosks, cafes, street corner society, and markets, moving around and about and outside the centers of absolutist administrative power. The urban masses do not occupy strategic positions in the economic system; but they are available for mass mobilizations capable of paralyzing the streets and plazas through which goods and services are transported out and profits are realized. Equally important, mass movements launched by the unemployed youth provide an opportunity for oppressed professionals, public sector employees, small business people and the self-employed to engage in protests without being subject to reprisals at their place of employment – dispelling the "fear factor" of losing one's job.

The political and social confrontation revolves around the opposite poles: clientelistic oligarchies and déclassé masses (the *Arab Street*). The former depend directly on the state (military/police apparatus) and the latter on amorphous local, informal, face-to-face improvised organizations. The exception is the minority of university students who move via the internet and the religious opposition, which finds ongoing focal points through their places of worship, both mosques and churches. Organized industrial trade unions come into the struggle late and largely focus on sectoral economic demands, with some exceptions - especially in public enterprises, controlled by cronies of the oligarchs, where workers demand changes in management. So while the distortions of the economy and the poverty this engenders provide an economic impetus for revolt, this does not facilitate a political consciousness directed so much at the structures of capitalism as at the imperialist domination of the country by the US.

As a result of the economic structuring of the rentier states, the uprisings do not take the form of class struggles between wage labor and industrial capitalists. They emerge as mass political revolts against the oligarchical state. Street-based social movements demonstrate their capacity to delegitimize state authority, paralyze the economy, and can lead up to the ousting of the ruling autocrats. But *it is the nature of mass street movements to fill the squares with relative ease, but also to be dispersed when the symbols of oppression are ousted.* Street-based movements lack the organization and leadership to project, let alone impose a new political or social order. Their power is found in their ability to pressure existing elites and institutions, not to replace the state and economy. Hence the surprising ease with which the US, Israeli and EU backed Egyptian military were able to seize power and protect the entire rentier state and economic structure while sustaining their ties with their imperial mentors, while giving an appearance of administering economic and political redress through a promise of prosecution for corruption of specific individuals and businessmen.

Converging Conditions and the "Demonstration Effect"

The spread of the Arab revolts across North Africa, the Middle East and Gulf States is, in the first instance, a product of similar historical and social conditions: rentier states ruled by family-clan oligarchs dependent on "rents" from capital intensive oil and energy exports, which confine the vast majority of youth to marginal, informal 'street-based' economic activities.

The "power of example" or the "demonstration effect" can only be understood by recognizing the same socio-political conditions in each country. Street power – mass urban movements – presumes the street as the economic locus of the principal actors and the takeover of the plazas as the place to exert political power and project social demands. No doubt the partial successes in Egypt and Tunisia did detonate the movements elsewhere. But they did so only in countries with the same historical legacy, the same social polarities between rentier – clan rulers and marginal street labor and especially where the rulers were deeply integrated and subordinated to imperial economic and military networks.

Conclusion

Rentier rulers govern via their ties to the US and EU military and financial institutions. They modernize their affluent enclaves and necessarily marginalize recently educated youth, who are confined to low paid jobs, especially in the insecure informal sector, centered in the streets of the capital cities, as there is no development of the economy. Neoliberal privatizations, reductions in public subsidies (for food, unemployment subsidies, cooking oil, gas, transport, health, and education) shattered the paternalistic ties through which the rulers contained the discontent of the young and poor, as well as clerical elites and tribal chiefs. The confluence of classes and masses, modern and traditional, was a direct result of a process of neoliberalization from above and exclusion from below. The neoliberal "reformers" promise that the 'market' would substitute well-paying jobs for the loss of state paternalistic subsidies was false. The neoliberal polices reinforced the concentration of wealth while weakening state controls over the masses.

The world capitalist economic crises led Europe and the US to tighten their immigration controls, eliminating one of the escape valves of the regimes – the massive flight of unemployed educated youth seeking jobs abroad. Out-migration was no longer an option; the choices narrowed to struggle or suffer. Studies show that those who emigrate tend to be the most ambitious, better educated (within their class) and greatest risk takers. Now, confined to their home country, with few illusions of overseas opportunities, they are forced to struggle for individual mobility at home through collective social and political action.

Equally important among the political youth, is the fact that the US, as guarantor of the rentier regimes, is seen as a declining imperial power: challenged economically in the world market by China; facing defeat as an occupying colonial ruler in Iraq and Afghanistan; and humiliated as a subservient and mendacious servant of an increasingly discredited Israel via its Zionist agents in the Obama regime and Congress. All of these elements of US imperial decay and discredit, encourage the pro-democracy movements to move forward against the US clients that are ruling their countries, and lessen their fears that the US military would intervene since it would face a third military front. The mass movements view their oligarchies as "third tier" regimes: rentier states under US hegemony, which, in turn, is under Israeli – Zionist tutelage. With 130 countries in the UN General Assembly and the entire Security Council, minus the US, condemning Israeli colonial expansion; with Lebanon, Egypt, Tunisia and the forthcoming new regimes in Yemen and Bahrain promising democratic foreign policies, the mass movements realize that all of Israel's modern arms and 680,000 soldiers are of no avail in the face of its total diplomatic isolation, its loss of regional rentier clients, and the utter discredit of its bombastic militarist rulers and their Zionist agents in the US diplomatic corps .[12]

The very socio-economic structures and political conditions which detonated the pro-democracy mass movements, the unemployed and underemployed youth organized from "the street", now present the greatest challenge: can the amorphous and diverse mass becomes an organized social and political force which can take state power, democratize the regime and, at the same time, create a new productive economy to provide stable well-paying employment, so far lacking in the rentier economy? The political outcome to date is indeterminate: democrats and socialists compete with clerical, monarchist, and neoliberal forces bankrolled by the U.S.

It is premature to celebrate a popular democratic revolution....

ENDNOTES

1   *Los Angeles Times*, Feb. 16, 2011.
2   *Daily Alert*, Feb. 25, 2011.
3   *Financial Times*, Feb. 22, 2011, p. 14.
4   *World Bank Annual Report*, 2009.
5   *Economic and Political Weekly*, Feb. 12, 2011, p. 11.
6   *Washington Blog*, Feb. 24, 2011.
7   *Financial Times*, Feb. 25, 2011, p. 1.
8   Ahmad Al-Sayed El-Naggar "US Aid to Europe: The Current and Future Situation," *Carnegie Endowment*, June, 2009, <http://www.carnegieendowment.org/publications/index.cfm?fa=view&id=23282>
9   *Economic and Political Weekly*, February 12, 2011, p. 11.
10   Id.
11   Washington Blog, February 24, 2011.
12   *Financial Times*, February 24, 2011, p. 7.

THE EURO-US WAR ON LIBYA

OFFICIAL LIES AND MISCONCEPTIONS OF CRITICS

JAMES PETRAS AND ROBIN E. ABAYA

Introduction

Many critics of the ongoing Euro-US wars in the Middle East, and now North Africa, have based their arguments on clichés and generalizations devoid of fact. The most common line heard in regard to the current US-Euro war on Libya is that it's "all about oil"—the goal is the seizure of Libya's oil wells.

On the other hand Euro–U.S, government spokespeople defend the war by claiming it's "all about saving civilian lives in the face of genocide", calling it "humanitarian intervention".

Following the lead of their imperial powers, most of what passes for the Left in the US and Europe, ranging from Social Democrats, Marxists, Trotskyists, Greens and other assorted progressives, claim they see and support a revolutionary mass uprising of the Libyan people, and not a few have called for military intervention by the imperial powers, or the same thing, the UN, to help the "Libyan revolutionaries" defeat the Gaddafi dictatorship.

These arguments are without foundation and belie the true nature of US-UK-French imperial power—*expansionist militarism*, as evidenced in all the *ongoing*

41

wars over the past decade (Iraq, Afghanistan, Somalia, etc.). What is much more revealing about the militarist intervention in Libya is that the major countries that refused to engage in the War operate via a very different form of global expansion based on economic and market forces. China, India, Brazil, Russia, Turkey and Germany, the most dynamic capitalist countries in Asia, Europe and the Middle East are fundamentally opposed to the self-styled "allied" military response against the Libyan government—because Gaddafi represents no threat to their security and they already have full access to the oil and a favorable investment climate. Besides, these economically dynamic countries see no prospect for a stable, progressive or democratic Libyan government emerging from the so-called 'rebel' leaders, who are disparate elites competing for power and Western favor.

(1) The Six Myths about Libya: Right and Left

The principal imperial powers and their mass media mouthpieces claim they are bombing Libya for "humanitarian reasons". Their recent past and current military interventions present a different picture: The intervention in Iraq resulted in well over a million civilian deaths, four million refugees and the systematic destruction of a complex society and its infrastructure, including its water supplies and sewage treatment, irrigation, electricity grid, factories, not to mention research centers, schools, historical archives, museums and Iraq's extensive social welfare system.

A worse disaster followed the invasion of Afghanistan. What was trumpeted as a 'humanitarian intervention' to liberate Afghan women and drive out the Taliban resulted in a human catastrophe for the Afghan people.

The road to imperial barbarism in Iraq began with 'sanctions', progressed to 'no fly zones', then de facto partition of the north, invasion and foreign occupation and the unleashing of sectarian warfare among the 'liberated' Iraqi death squads.

Equally telling, the imperial assault against Yugoslavia in the 1990's, trotted out as the great "humanitarian war" to stop genocide, led to a 40-day aerial bombardment and destruction of Belgrade and other major cities, the imposition of a gangster terrorist regime (KLA) in Kosovo, the near-total ethnic cleansing of all non-Albanian residents from Kosovo and the construction of the largest US military base on the continent (Camp Bondsteel).

The bombing of Libya has already destroyed major civilian infrastructure, airports, roads, seaports and communication centers, as well as 'military' targets. The blockade of Libya and military attacks have driven out scores of multinational corporations and led to the mass exodus of hundreds of thousands of Asian, Eastern European, Sub-Saharan African, Middle Eastern and North African skilled and unskilled immigrant workers and specialists of all types, devastating the economy and creating, virtually overnight, massive unemployment, bread lines and critical gasoline shortages. Moreover, following the logic of previous imperial military interventions, the seemingly 'restrained' call to patrol the skies via "no fly zone", has led directly to bombing civilian as well as military targets on the ground, and to pushing to overthrow the legitimate government. The current imperial warmongers leading the attack on Libya, just like their predecessors, are not engaged in anything remotely resembling a humanitarian mission: they are destroying the fundamental basis of the civilian lives they claim to be saving—or as an earlier generation of American generals would claim in Vietnam, they are 'destroying the villages in order to save them'.

(2) War for Oil or Oil for Sale?

The 'critical' Left's favorite cliché is that the imperial

invasion is all about "seizing control of Libya's oil and turning it over to their multinationals". This is despite the fact that US, French and British multinationals (as well as their Asian competitors) had already "taken over" millions of acres of Libyan oil fields without dropping a single bomb. For the past decade, "Big Oil" had been pumping and exporting Libyan oil and gas and reaping huge profits. Gaddafi welcomed the biggest MNCs to exploit the oil wealth of Libya from the early 1990s to the present day. There are more major oil companies doing business in Libya than in most oil-producing regions in the world. These include: British Petroleum, with a seven-year contract on two concessions and over $1 billion dollars in planned investments. Each BP concession exploits huge geographic areas of Libya, one the size of Kuwait and the other the size of Belgium.[1] In addition, five Japanese major corporations, including Mitsubishi and Nippon Petroleum, Italy's Eni Gas, British Gas and the US giant Exxon Mobil signed new exploration and exploitation contracts in October 2010. The most recent oil concession signed in January 2010 mainly benefited US oil companies, especially Occidental Petroleum. Other multinationals operating in Libya include Royal Dutch Shell, Total (France), Oil India, CNBC (China), Indonesia's Pertamina and Norway's Norsk Hydro.[2]

Despite the economic sanctions against Libya imposed by US President Reagan in 1986, US multinational giant, Halliburton, had secured multi-billion dollar gas and oil projects since the 1980s. During his tenure as CEO of Halliburton, former Defense Secretary Cheney led the fight against these sanctions, stating, "as a nation (there is) enormous value having American businesses engaged around the world".[3] Officially, sanctions against Libya were only lifted under Bush in 2004. Clearly, with all the European and US imperial countries already exploiting Libya oil on a massive scale, the mantra that the "war is about oil" doesn't hold water or oil!

(3) Gaddafi is a Terrorist

In the run-up to the current military assault on Tripoli, the US Treasury Department's (and Israel's special agent) Stuart Levey authored a sanctions policy freezing $30 billion dollars in Libyan assets on the pretext that Gaddafi was a murderous tyrant.[4] However, seven years earlier, Cheney, Bush and Condoleezza Rice had taken Libya off the list of terrorist regimes and ordered Levey and his minions to lift the Reagan-era sanctions. Every major European power quickly followed suit: Gaddafi was welcomed in European capitals, prime ministers visited Tripoli and Gaddafi reciprocated by unilaterally dismantling his nuclear and chemical weapons programs.[5] Gaddafi became Washington's partner in its campaign against a broad array of groups, political movements and individuals arbitrarily placed on the US "terror list", arresting, torturing and killing Al Qaeda suspects, expelling Palestinian militants and openly criticizing Hezbollah, Hamas and other opponents of Israel probably for their support of an Islam-based opposition in Libya. The United Nations Human Rights Commission gave the Gaddafi regime a clean bill of health in 2010. In the end Gaddafi's political 'turnabout', however much profited from and celebrated by the Western elite, did not save him from this massive military assault. The imposition of neoliberal 'reforms', his political 'apostasy' and cooperation in the 'War on Terror' and his acceptance to terminate the pursuit of Libyan nuclear weapons, only weakened the regime. Libya became vulnerable to attack and isolated from any consequential anti-imperialist allies except perhaps, Chavez and ALBA. Gaddafi's concessions to the West set his regime up as an easy target for the militarists of Washington, London and Paris, eager for a quick 'victory'.

(4) The Myth of the Revolutionary Masses

The Left, including the mainly electoral social democrat, green and even left-socialist parties of Europe and the US swallowed the entire mass media propaganda package demonizing the Gaddafi regime while lauding the 'rebels'. Parroting their imperial mentors and swallowing a barrage of deceptive media misinformation, the 'Left' justified their support for imperial military intervention in the name of the "revolutionary Libyan people", the "peace-loving" masses "fighting tyranny" and organizing peoples' militias to "liberate their country". Nothing could be further from the truth.

The center of the armed uprising is Benghazi, longtime monarchist hotbed of tribal supporters and clients of the deposed King Idris and his family. Idris, until he was overthrown by the young firebrand Col. Gaddafi, had ruled Libya with an iron fist over a semi-feudal backwater and was popular with Washington, having given the US its largest air base (Wheeler) in the Mediterranean. Among the feuding leaders of the "transitional council" in Benghazi (who purport to lead but have few organized followers) one finds neoliberal expats, who first promoted the Euro-US military invasion envisioning their ride to power on the back of Western missiles .They openly favor dismantling the Libyan state oil companies currently engaged in joint ventures with foreign MNCs. Independent observers have commented on the lack of any clear reformist tendencies, let alone revolutionary organizations or democratic popular movements among the 'rebels'. Even the head of AFRICOM does not really know who these "REBELS" are—or perhaps more accurately, who will emerge as the dominant party among same—the US-favored neoliberals, monarchists and proxies, or the Islamist wing with its own agenda.

While the US, British and French are firing missiles, loaded with depleted uranium, at the Libyan military and key civilian installations, their 'allies' the armed militias in Benghazi, rather than go to battle against the regime's armed forces, are busy rounding up, arresting and often executing any suspected members of Gaddafi's "revolutionary committees", arbitrarily labeling these civilians as "fifth columnists". The top leaders of these "revolutionary" masses in Benghazi include two recent defectors from what the 'Left' dubs Gaddafi's "murderous regime": Mustafa Abdul Jalil, a former Justice minister, who prosecuted dissenters up to the day before the armed uprising, Mahmoud Jabril, who was prominent in inviting multinationals to take over the oil fields,[6] and Gaddafi's former ambassador to India, Ali Aziz al-Eisawa, who jumped ship as soon as it looked like the uprising appeared to be succeeding. These self-appointed 'leaders' of the rebels who now staunchly support the Euro-US military intervention, were long-time supporters of the Gaddafis'dictatorship and promoters of MNC takeovers of oil and gas fields. At first, the heads of the "rebels" military council were Omar Hariri and General Abdul Fattah Younis, former head of the Ministry of Interior. Both men have long histories (since 1969) of repressing democratic movements within Libya. There had been a virtual ban in the US media on reporting the name of Khalifa Haftar, the long-time CIA collaborator who was appointed chief rebel commander March 17, on the eve of the US-NATO bombing campaign against Libya.[7] Haftar and Younis were engaged in a bitter rivalry, which it seems at this writing that Younis has won. Given their unsavory background, it is not surprising that these top level military defectors to the 'rebel' cause have been unable to arouse their troops, mostly conscripts, to engage the loyalist forces backing Gaddafi. They too will have to take ride into Tripoli on the coattails of the Anglo-US-French armed forces.

The anti-Gaddafi force's lack of any democratic credentials and mass support is evident in their reliance on foreign imperial armed forces to bring them to power and their subservience to imperial demands. Their abuse and persecution of immigrant workers from Asia, Turkey and especially sub-Sahara Africa, as well as black Libyan citizens, is well documented in the international press. Their brutal treatment of black Libyans, falsely accused of being Gaddafi's "mercenaries" , includes torture, mutilation and horrific executions, does not auger well for the advent of a new democratic order, or even the revival of an economy, which has been dependent on immigrant labor, let alone a unified country with national institutions and a *national* economy.

The self-declared leadership of the "National Transitional Council" is not democratic, nationalist or even capable of uniting the country. These are not credible leaders capable of restoring the economy and creating jobs lost as a result of their armed power grab. No one seriously envisions these 'exiles', tribalists, monarchists and Islamists maintaining the paternalistic social welfare and employment programs created by the Gaddafi government and which gave Libyans the highest per-capita income in Africa.

Most likely the imperial powers never intended to "create a democratic welfare state—an electoral version of gaddafism—in any event, but simply to divide yet another African country in a manner which might be described as "oil plus some surrounding territory"—much as was accomplished in the Sudan and earlier in the Middle East with the Emirates—as a side-bonus at least, to the military empire building, which has to ultimately be justified by an economic payoff to the corporate elite.

(5) Al Qaeda

The greatest geographical concentration of suspected terrorists with links to Al Qaeda just happens to be in the areas dominated by the "rebels".[8] For over a decade Gaddafi has been in the forefront of the fight against Al Qaeda, following his embrace of the Bush-Obama 'War on Terror' doctrine. These jihadist Libyans, having honed their skills in US-occupied Iraq and Afghanistan, are now among the ranks of the "rebels" fighting the much more secular Libyan government. Likewise, the tribal chiefs, fundamentalist clerics and monarchists in the East have been active in a "holy war" against Gaddafi welcoming arms and air support from the Anglo-French-US "crusaders"—just like the mullahs and tribal chiefs welcomed the arms and training from the Carter-Reagan White House to overthrow a secular regime in Afghanistan: a marriage of convenience between western imperialists and Islamic nationalists Once again, imperial intervention is based on 'alliances' with the most retrograde forces. The composition of the future regime (or regimes, if Libya is divided) is a big question and the prospects of a return to political stability for Big Oil to profitably exploit Libya's resources are dubious.

(6) "Genocide" or Armed Civil War

Unlike all ongoing mass popular Arab uprisings, the Libyan conflict began as an *armed* insurrection, directed at seizing power by force. Unlike the autocratic rulers of Egypt and Tunisia, Gaddafi has secured a mass regional base among a substantial sector of the Libyan population. This support is based on the fact that almost two generations of Libyans have benefited from Gaddafi's petroleum-financed welfare, educational, employment and housing programs, none of which existed under America's favorite, King Idris. Since violence is inherent in any armed uprising, once one picks up the gun to seize power, they lose their claim on 'civil rights'. In armed civil conflicts, civil rights are violated on all sides. Regardless of the Western media's lurid portrayal of Gaddafi's "African mercenary forces" and its more muted approval of 'revolutionary justice' against Gaddafi supporters and government soldiers captured in the rebel strongholds, the rules of warfare should have come into play, including the protection of non-combatants-civilians (including government supporters and officials), as well as protection of Libyan prisoners of war in the areas under NATO-rebel control.

The unsubstantiated Euro-US claim of "genocide" amplified by the mass media and parroted by "left" spokespersons is contradicted by the daily reports of single and double digit deaths and injuries, resulting from urban violence on both sides, as control of cities and towns shifts between the two sides.

Truth is the first casualty of war, and especially of civil war. Both sides have resorted to monstrous fabrications of victories, casualties, monsters and victims.

Demons and angels aside, this conflict began as a civil war between two sets of Libyan elites: An established paternalistic, now burgeoning neoliberal, autocracy with substantial popular backing versus a western imperialist-financed and trained elite, backed by an amorphous group of regional, tribal and clerical chiefs, monarchists and neoliberal professionals devoid of democratic and nationalist credentials—and lacking broad-based mass support.

Conclusion

If not to prevent genocide, grab the oil or promote democracy (via Patriot missiles), what then is the driving force behind the Euro-US imperial intervention?

A clue is in the selectivity of Western military intervention: In Bahrain, Saudi Arabia, Yemen, Jordan, Qatar and Oman, ruling autocrats allied with and backed by Euro-US imperial states go about arresting, torturing and murdering unarmed urban protestors with total impunity.

In Egypt and Tunisia, the US is backing a conservative junta of self-appointed civil-military elites in order to block the profound democratic and nationalist transformation of society demanded by the protesters. The 'junta' aims to push through neoliberal economic "reforms" through carefully-vetted pro-Western 'elected' officials. While liberal critics may accuse the West of "hypocrisy" and "double standards" in bombing Gaddafi but not the Gulf butchers, in reality the imperial rulers consistently apply the *same standards* in each region: They defend *strategic autocratic client regimes*, which have allowed imperial states to build strategic air force and naval bases, run regional intelligence operations and set up logistical platforms for their ongoing wars in Iraq and Afghanistan as well as their future planned conflict with Iran. They attack Gaddafi's Libya precisely because Gaddafi had refused to actively contribute to Western military operations in Africa and the Middle East.

The key point is that while Libya allows the biggest US-European multinationals to plunder its oil wealth, it *did not become a strategic geo-political-military asset of the empire*. As we have written in many previous essays the driving force of US empire-building is *military—and not economic*.[10] This is why billions of dollars of Western economic interests and contracts had been sacrificed in the setting up of sanctions against Iraq and Iran—with the costly result that the invasion and occupation of Iraq shut down most oil exploitation for over a decade.

The Washington-led assault on Libya, with the majority of air sorties and missiles strikes being carried out by the Obama regime, is part of a more general counter-attack in response to the most recent Arab popular pro-democracy movements. The West is backing the suppression of these pro-democracy movements throughout the Gulf; it finances the pro-imperial, pro-Israel junta in Egypt and it is intervening in Tunisia to ensure that any new regime is "correctly aligned". It supports a despotic regime in Algeria as well as Israel's daily assaults on Gaza. In line with this policy, the West backs the uprising of ex-Gaddafites and right-wing monarchists, confident that the 'liberated' Libya will once again provide military bases for the US-European military empire-builders.

In contrast, the emerging market-driven global and regional powers have refused to support this conflict, which jeopardizes their access to oil and threatens the current large-scale oil exploration contracts signed with Gaddafi. The growing economies of Germany, China, Russia, Turkey, India and Brazil rely on exploiting new markets and natural resources all over Africa and the Middle East, while the US, Britain and France spend billions pursuing wars that de-stabilize these markets, destroy infrastructure and foment long-term wars of resistance. The growing market powers recognize that the Libyan "rebels" cannot secure a quick victory or ensure a stable environment for long-term trade and investments. But more importantly, the "rebels", once in power, will be political clients of their militarist imperial mentors. Clearly, imperial military intervention on behalf of regional separatists seriously threatens these emerging market powers' economies: The US supports ethno-religious rebels in China's Tibetan province and as well as the Uyghur separatists; Washington and London have long backed the Chechen separatists in the Russian Caucuses. India is wary of the US military support for Pakistan, which claims Kashmir. Turkey is facing Kurdish separatists who receive arms and safe haven from their US-supplied Iraqi Kurdish counterparts.

The North African precedent of an imperial invasion of Libya on behalf of its separatist clients worries the emerging market-powers. It is also an ongoing threat to the mass-based popular Arab freedom movements. And the invasion sounds the death knell for the US economy and its fragile 'recovery', even if ostensibly palmed off on NATO. With CIA boots on the ground in Libya, and with US moving forward on Africom, it is hard to believe that military empire in Africa is now on a back burner.

But three ongoing, endless wars will break the budget much sooner than later.

ENDNOTES

1   *Libyonline.com*.
2   BBC News, October 3, 2005.
3   *Halliburtonwatch.com*.
4   *Washington Post*, March 24, 2011.
5   BBC, September 5, 2008
6   *Financial Times*, March 23, 2011, p. 7.
7   Patrick Martin, "Mounting Evidence of CIA Ties to Rebels," *wsws.org*, April 4, 2011, <http://www.wsws.org/articles/2011/apr2011/liby-a04.shtml>
8   See Alexander Cockburn: *Counterpunch*, March 24, 2011.
9   See in particular, "Military Over Market-Driven Empire Building, 1950-2008" in James Petras, *Zionism, Militarism and the Decline of US Power*, Clarity Press, Inc., 2008.

LIBYA AND OBAMA'S DEFENSE OF THE 'REBEL UPRISING'

Over the past two weeks Libya has been subjected to the most brutal imperial air, sea and land assault in its modern history. Thousands of bombs and missiles, launched from American and European submarines, warships and fighter planes, are destroying Libyan military bases, airports, roads, ports, oil depots, artillery emplacements, tanks, armored carriers, planes and troop concentrations. Dozens of CIA and SAS special forces have been training, advising and mapping targets for the so-called Libyan 'rebels' engaged in a civil war against the Gaddafi government, its armed forces, popular militias and civilian supporters.[1]

Despite this massive military support and their imperial 'allies' total control of Libya's sky and coastline, the 'rebels' have proven incapable of mobilizing village or town support and are in retreat after being confronted by the Libyan government's highly motivated troops and village militias.[2]

One of the most flimsy excuse for this inglorious rebel retreat offered by the Cameron-Obama-Sarkozy 'coalition', echoed by the mass media, is that their Libyan 'clients' are "outgunned".[3] Obviously Obama and company don't count the scores of jets, dozens of warships and submarines, the hundreds of daily attacks and the thousands of bombs dropped on the Libyan government since the start of Western imperial intervention. Direct military intervention of 20 major and minor foreign military powers, savaging the sovereign Libyan state, as well as scores of political accomplices in the United Nations do not contribute to any military advantage for the imperial clients–according to the daily pro-rebel propaganda. The *Los Angeles Times* (March 31, 2011), however described how "...*many rebels in gun-mounted trucks turned and fled...even though their heavy machine guns and antiaircraft guns seemed a match for any similar government vehicle.*" Indeed, no 'rebel' force in recent history has received such sustained military support from so many imperial powers in their confrontation with an established regime. Nevertheless, at this writing, the 'rebel' forces on the front lines are in full retreat, fleeing in disarray and thoroughly disgusted with their 'rebel' generals and ministers back in Benghazi. Meanwhile the 'rebel' leaders, in elegant suits and tailored uniforms, answer the 'call to battle' by attending 'summits' in London where the 'liberation strategy' consists of their appeal before the mass media for imperial ground troops.[4]

Morale among the frontline 'rebels' is low: According to credible reports from the battlefront at Ajdabiya, "*Rebels ...complained that their erstwhile commanders were nowhere to be found. They griped about comrades who fled to the relative safety of Benghazi...(they complained that) forces in Benghazi monopolized 400 donated field radios and 400 more...satellite phones intended for the battlefield... (mostly) rebels say commanders rarely visit the battlefield and exercise little authority because many fighters do not trust them*".[5] Apparently 'Twitter' doesn't work on the battlefield.

The decisive issues in a the civil war are not weapons, training or leadership, although certainly these factors are important: The basic difference between the military capability of the pro-government Libyan forces and the

Libyan 'rebels', backed by both Western imperialists and 'progressives,' lies in their motivation, values and material advances. Western imperialist intervention has heightened *national consciousness* among the Libyan people, who now view their confrontation with the anti-Gaddafi 'rebels' as a fight to defend their homeland from foreign air and sea power and puppet land troops—a powerful incentive for any people or army. The opposite is true for the 'rebels', whose leaders have surrendered their national identity and depend entirely on imperialist military intervention to put them in power. What rank and file 'rebel' fighters are going to risk their lives, fighting their own compatriots, just to place their country under an imperialist or neo-colonial rule?

Finally Western journalists' accounts are coming to light of village and town pro-government militias repelling these 'rebels' and even how *"a busload of (Libyan) women suddenly emerged (from one village)...and began cheering as though they supported the rebels..."* drawing the Western-backed rebels into a deadly ambush set by their pro-government husbands and neighbors.[6]

The 'rebels', who enter their villages, are seen as invaders, breaking doors, blowing up homes and arresting and accusing local leaders of being 'fifth columnists' for Gaddafi, an absurd deployment of the term, in the circumstances. The threat of military 'rebel' occupation, the arrest and abuse of local authorities and the disruption of highly valued family, clan and local community relations have motivated local Libyan militias and fighters to attack the Western-backed 'rebels'. The 'rebels' are regarded as 'outsiders' in terms of regional and clan allegiances; by trampling on local mores, the 'rebels' now find themselves in 'hostile' territory. What 'rebel' fighter would be willing to die defending hostile terrain? Such 'rebels' have only to call on foreign air-power to 'liberate' the pro-government village for them.

The Western media, unable to grasp these material advances by the pro-government forces, attribute popular backing of Gaddafi to 'coercion' or 'co-optation', relying on 'rebel' claims that 'everybody is *secretly* opposed to the regime'. There is another *material reality*, which is conveniently ignored: The Gaddafi regime has effectively used the country's oil wealth to build a vast network of public schools, hospitals and clinics. Libyans have the highest *per capita* income in Africa at $14,900 per annum.[7] Tens of thousands of low-income Libyan students have received scholarships to study at home and overseas. The urban infrastructure has been modernized, agriculture is subsidized and small-scale producers and manufacturers receive government credit. Gaddafi has overseen these effective programs, in addition to enriching his own clan/family. Much of "Gaddafi's billions" frozen in foreign banks are in actuality primarily the assets of the Libyan Central Bank and its sovereign investment fund, and not run by Gaddafi.. On the other hand, the Libyan rebels and their imperial mentors have targeted the entire civilian economy, bombed Libyan cities, cut trade and commercial networks, blocked the delivery of subsidized food and welfare to the poor, caused the suspension of schools and forced hundreds of thousands of foreign professionals, teachers, doctors and skilled contract workers to flee.

Libyans, who might otherwise resent Gaddafi's long authoritarian tenure, are now faced with the choice between supporting an advanced, functioning welfare state or a foreign-directed military conquest. Many have chosen, quite rationally, to stand with the regime.

The debacle of the imperial-backed 'rebel' forces, despite their immense technical-military advantage, is due to the *quisling* leadership, their role as 'internal colonialists' invading local communities and above all their wanton destruction of a social-welfare system which has benefited millions of ordinary Libyans for two generations. The failure of the 'rebels' to advance, despite the massive support of imperial air and sea power, means that the US-France-Britain 'coalition' will have to escalate its intervention beyond sending special forces, advisers and CIA assassination teams. Given Obama-Clinton's stated objective of 'regime change', there will be no choice but to introduce imperialist troops, send large-scale shipments of armored carriers and tanks, and increase the use of the highly destructive depleted uranium munitions.

No doubt Obama, the most public face of 'humanitarian armed intervention' in Africa, will recite bigger and more grotesque lies, as Libyan villagers and townspeople fall victims to his imperial juggernaut. Washington's 'first black Chief Executive' will earn history's infamy as the US President responsible for the slaughter of hundreds of black Libyans and mass expulsion of millions of sub-Saharan African workers employed under the current regime.[8]

No doubt, Anglo-American progressives and leftists will continue to debate (in 'civilized tones') the pros and cons of this 'intervention', following in the footsteps of their predecessors, the French Socialists and US New Dealers from the 1930s, who once debated the pros and cons of supporting Republican Spain... while Hitler and Mussolini bombed the republic on behalf of the 'rebel' fascist forces under General Franco who upheld the Falangist banner of 'Family, Church and Civilization'—a fascist prototype for Obama's 'humanitarian intervention' on behalf of his 'rebels'.

ENDNOTES

1   *The New York Times*, March 30, 2011.

2   Al Jazeera, March 30, 2011.
3   *Financial Times*, March 29, 2011.
4   *The Independent* (London) March 31, 2011.
5   *Los Angeles Times*, March 31, 2011.
6   *Globe and Mail* (Canada) March 28, 2011 and *McClatchy NewsService*, March 29, 2011
7   *Financial Times*, April 2, 2011.
8   *Globe and Mail*, March 28, 2011.

CONTEXTUALIZING THE 'ARAB SPRING'

NETWORKS OF EMPIRE AND REALIGNMENTS OF WORLD POWER

Imperial states build networks which link economic, military and political activities into a coherent, mutually reinforcing system. This task is largely performed by the various institutions of the imperial state. Thus imperial action is not always *directly* economic, as military action in one country or region is necessary to open or protect economic zones. Nor are all military actions decided by economic interests if the leading sector of the imperial state is decidedly militarist.

Moreover, the *sequence* of imperial action may vary according to the particular conditions necessary for empire building. Thus state aid may buy collaborators; military intervention may secure client regimes to be followed later by private investors. In other circumstances, the entry of private corporations may precede state intervention.

In either private or state economic and/or military-led penetration in furtherance of empire-building, the strategic purpose is to exploit the special economic and geopolitical features of the targeted country to create empire-centered networks. In the post Eurocentric colonial world, the privileged position of the US in its empire-centered policies, treaties, trade and military agreements is disguised and justified by an ideological gloss, which varies with time and circumstances. In the war to break-up Yugoslavia and establish client regimes, as in Kosovo, imperial ideology utilized humanitarian rhetoric. In the genocidal wars in the Middle East, anti-terrorism and anti-Islamic ideology is central. Against China, democratic and human rights rhetoric predominates. In Latin America, receding imperial power relies on democratic and anti-authoritarian rhetoric aimed at the democratically elected Chavez government.

The effectiveness of imperial ideology is in direct relation to the capacity of empire to promote viable and dynamic development alternatives *to their targeted countries*. By that criteria, imperial ideology has had little persuasive power among target populations. The Islamophobic and anti-terrorist rhetoric has made no impact on the peoples of the Middle East and alienated the Islamic world. Latin America's lucrative trade relations with the Chavist government and the decline of the US economy has undermined Washington's ideological campaign to isolate Venezuela. The US human rights campaign against China has been totally ignored not only throughout the EU, Africa, Latin America, and Oceana but by the 500 biggest US MNC (and even by the US Treasury, busy selling treasury bonds to China to finance the ballooning US budget deficit).

The weakening influence of imperial propaganda and the declining economic leverage of Washington means that the US imperial networks built over the past half century are being eroded or at least subjected to centrifugal forces. Former fully integrated networks in Asia are now merely military bases as the local economies secure greater autonomy and orient toward China and beyond. In other words, the imperial networks are now being transformed into limited operations' outposts, rather than centers for imperial economic plunder.

Imperial Networks: The Central Role of Collaborators

Empire-building is essentially a process of penetrating

a country or region, establishing a privileged position and retaining control in order to (1) secure lucrative resources, markets and cheap labor (2) establish a military platform to expand into adjoining countries and regions (3) establish military bases to establish a chokehold over strategic road or waterways to deny or limit internal access of competitors or adversaries, and (4) set up intelligence and clandestine operations against adversaries and competitors.

History has demonstrated that the lowest cost means of sustaining long term, large- scale imperial domination is by developing local collaborators, whether in the form of political, economic and/or military leaders operating from client regimes. Overt politico-military imperial rule results in costly wars and disruption, especially among a broad array of classes adversely affected by the imperial presence.

The formation of collaborator rulers and classes results from diverse short and long term imperial policies ranging from direct military, electoral and extra-parliamentary activities to middle to long term recruitment, training and orientation of promising young leaders via propaganda and educational programs, cultural-financial inducements, promises of political and economic backing on assuming political office and through substantial clandestine financial backing.

The most basic appeal by imperial policymakers to the "new ruling class" in emerging client state is the opportunity to participate in an economic system tied to the imperial centers, in which local elites share economic wealth with their imperial benefactors as well as a sense of personal identification with the global elite. To secure mass support, the collaborator classes obfuscate the new forms of imperial subservience and economic exploitation by emphasizing political independence, personal freedom, economic opportunity and private consumerism.

The mechanisms for the transfer of power to an emerging client state combine imperial propaganda, financing of mass organizations and electoral parties, as well as violent coups or 'popular uprisings'. Authoritarian bureaucratically ossified regimes relying on police controls to limit or oppose imperial expansion are "soft targets". Selective human rights campaigns become the most effective organizational weapon to recruit activists and promote leaders for the imperial-centered new political order. Once the power transfer takes place, the former members of the political, economic and cultural elite are banned, repressed, arrested and jailed. A new *homogenous political culture of competing parties embracing the imperial centered world order* emerges. The first order of business beyond the political purge is the privatization and handover of the commanding heights of the economy to imperial enterprises. The client regimes proceed to provide soldiers to engage as paid mercenaries in imperial wars and to transfer military bases to imperial forces as platforms of intervention. The entire "independence charade" is accompanied by the massive dismantling of public social welfare programs (pensions, free health and education), labor codes and full employment policies. Promotion of a highly polarized class structure is the ultimate consequence of client rule. The imperial-centered economies of the client regimes, as a replica of any commonplace satrap state, is justified (or legitimated) in the name of an electoral system dubbed democratic—in fact a political system dominated by new capitalist elites and their heavily funded mass media.

Imperial centered regimes run by collaborating elites spanning the Baltic States, Central and Eastern Europe to the Balkans is the most striking example of imperial expansion in the 20th century. The breakup of the Soviet Union and takeover of the Eastern bloc and its incorporation into the US led NATO alliance and the European Union resulted in imperial hubris. Washington made premature declarations of a unipolar world while Western Europe proceeded to plunder public resources, ranging from factories to real estate, exploiting cheap labor overseas and via immigration, drawing on a formidable 'reserve army' to undermine living standards of unionized labor in the West.

The unity of purpose of European and US imperial regimes allowed for the peaceful joint takeover of the wealth of the new regions by private monopolies. The imperial states initially subsidized the new client regimes with large scale transfers and loans on condition that they allowed imperial firms to seize resources, real estate, land, factories, service sectors, media outlets, etc. Heavily indebted states went from a sharp crises in the initial period to 'spectacular' growth and then to profound and chronic social crises with double digit unemployment in the 20 year period of client building. While worker protests emerged as wages deteriorated, unemployment soared and welfare provisions were cut, destitution spread. However the 'new middle class' embedded in the political and media apparatuses and in joint economic ventures are sufficiently funded by imperial financial institutions to protect their dominance.

The dynamic of imperial expansion in East, Central and Southern Europe, however, did not provide the impetus for strategic advance, because of the ascendancy of highly volatile financial capital and a powerful militarist caste in the Euro-American political centers. In important respects, military and political expansion was no longer harnessed to economic conquest. The reverse was true: economic plunder and political dominance served as instruments enabling the projection of military power.

Imperial Sequences:
From War for Exploitation to Exploitation for War

The relations between imperial military policies and economic interests are complex and changing over time and historical context. In some circumstances, an imperial regime will invest heavily in military personnel and augment monetary expenditures to overthrow an anti-imperialist ruler and establish a client regime far beyond any state or private economic return. For example, US wars in Iraq and Afghanistan, and its proxy wars in Somalia and Yemen have not resulted in greater profits for US multinational corporations nor have they enhanced private exploitation of raw materials, labor or markets. At best, imperial wars have provided profits for mercenary contractors, construction companies and related 'war industries' profiting through transfers from the US treasury and the exploitation of US taxpayers, mostly wage and salary earners.

In many cases, especially after the Second World War, the emerging US imperial state lavished a multi-billion dollar loan and aid program for Western Europe. The Marshall Plan forestalled anti-capitalist social upheavals and restored capitalist political dominance. This allowed for the emergence of NATO (a military alliance led and dominated by the US). Subsequently, US multi-national corporations invested in and traded with Western Europe reaping lucrative profits, once the imperial state created favorable political and economic conditions. In other words imperial state politico-military intervention *preceded* the rise and expansion of US multinational capital. A myopic short term analysis of the initial post-war activity would downplay the importance of private US economic interests as the driving force of US policy. Extending the time period to the following two decades, the interplay between initial high cost state military and economic expenditures with later private high return gains provides a perfect example of how the process of imperial power operates.

The role of the imperial state as an instrument for opening, protecting and expanding private market, labor and resource exploitation corresponds to a time in which both the state and the dominant classes were primarily motivated by industrial empire building.

US directed military intervention and coups in Iran (1953), Guatemala (1954), Chile (1973), and the Dominican Republic (1965) were linked to specific imperial economic interests and corporations. For example, US and English oil corporations sought to reverse the nationalization of oil in Iran. The US and United Fruit Company opposed the agrarian reform policies in Guatemala. The major US copper and telecommunication companies supported and called for the US backed coup in Chile.

In contrast, current US military interventions and wars in the Middle East, South Asia and the Horn of Africa are not promoted by US multinationals. These imperial policies are promoted by militarists and Zionists embedded in the state, mass media and powerful 'civil' organizations. The same imperial methods (coups and wars) serve different imperial rulers and interests.

Clients, Allies and Puppet Regimes

Imperial networks involve securing a variety of complementary economic, military and political 'resource bases' which are both *part* of the imperial system and retain varying degrees of political and economic autonomy.

In the dynamic earlier stages of US Empire building, from roughly the 1950s–1970s, US multinational corporations and the economy as a whole dominated the world economy. Its allies in Europe and Asia were highly dependent on US markets, financing and development. US military hegemony was reflected in a series of regional military pacts which secured almost instant support for US regional wars, military coups and the construction of military bases and naval ports on their territory. Countries were divided into 'specializations' which served the particular interests of the US Empire. Western Europe was a military outpost, industrial partner and ideological collaborator. Asia, primarily Japan and South Korea served as 'frontline military outposts', as well as industrial partners. Indonesia, Malaysia, the Philippines were essentially client regimes which provided raw materials as well as military bases. Singapore and Hong Kong were financial and commercial entrepôts. Pakistan was a client military regime serving as a frontline pressure on China.

Saudi Arabia, Iran and the Gulf mini-states, ruled by client authoritarian regimes, provided oil and military bases. Egypt, Jordan and Israel anchored imperial interests in the Middle East. Beirut served as the financial center for US, European and Middle East bankers.

Africa and Latin America, including client and nationalist-populist regimes, were a source of raw materials as well as markets for finished goods and cheap labor.

The prolonged US-Vietnam war and Washington's subsequent defeat eroded the power of the empire. Western Europe, Japan and South Korea's industrial expansion challenged US industrial primacy. Latin America's pursuit of nationalist, import-substitution policies forced US investment toward overseas manufacturing. In the Middle East, nationalist movements toppled US clients in Iran and Iraq and undermined military outposts. Revolutions in Angola, Namibia, Mozambique, Algeria, Nicaragua and elsewhere curtailed Euro-American 'open ended' access to raw materials, at least temporarily.

The decline of the US Empire was temporarily arrested by the collapse of Communism in the Soviet Union and Eastern Europe, and the establishment of client regimes throughout the region. Likewise the upsurge of imperial-centered client regimes in Latin America between the mid 1970s to the end of the 1990s gave the appearance of an imperialist recovery. The 1990s, however, was not the beginning of a repeat of the early 1950s imperial take off: it was the "last hurrah" before a long term, irreversible decline. The entire imperial political apparatus, so successful in its clandestine operations in subverting the Soviet and Eastern

European regimes, played a marginal role when it came to capitalizing on the economic opportunities which ensued. Germany and other EU countries led the way in the takeover of lucrative privatized enterprises. Russian oligarchs (seven of the top eight became Israeli citizens) seized and pillaged privatized strategic industries, banks and natural resources. The principal US beneficiaries were the banks and Wall Street firms which laundered billions of illicit earnings and collected lucrative fees from mergers, acquisitions, stock listings and other less than transparent activities. In other words, the collapse of Soviet collectivism strengthened the parasitical financial sector of the US Empire. Worse still, the assumption of a 'unipolar world' fostered by US ideologues played into the hands of the militarists, who now assumed that former constraints on US military assaults on nationalists and Soviet allies had disappeared. As a result military intervention became the *principal* driving force in US empire building, leading to the first Iraq war, the Yugoslav and Somali invasion, and the expansion of US military bases throughout the former Soviet bloc and Eastern Europe.

At the very pinnacle of US global-political and military power during the 1990s, with all the major Latin American regimes enveloped in the empire-centered neoliberal warp, the seeds of decay and decline set in.

The economic crises of the late 1990s led to major uprisings and electoral defeats of practically all US clients in Latin America, spelling the decline of US imperial domination. China's extraordinary dynamic and cumulative growth displaced US manufacturing capital and weakened US leverage over rulers in Asia, Africa and Latin America. The vast transfer of US state resources to overseas imperial adventures, military bases and the shoring up of clients and allies led to domestic decline.

The US empire, passively facing economic competitors displacing the US in vital markets and engaged in prolonged and unending wars which drained the treasury, attracted a cohort of mediocre policymakers who lacked a coherent strategy for rectifying policies and reconstructing the state to serve productive activity capable of 'retaking markets'. Instead the policies of open-ended and unsustainable wars played into the hands of a special sub-group (sui generis) of militarists, American Zionists. They capitalized on their infiltration of strategic positions in the state, enhanced their influence in the mass media and through a vast network of organized "pressure groups" to reinforce US subordination to Israel's drive for Middle East supremacy.

The result was the total "unbalancing" of the US imperial apparatus: *military action was unhinged from economic empire building.* A highly influential upper caste of Zionist-militarists harnessed US military power to an economically marginal state (Israel), in perpetual hostility toward the 1.5 billion Muslim world. Equally damaging, American Zionist ideologues and policymakers promoted repressive institutions, legislation and Islamophobic ideological propaganda designed to *terrorize* the US population. Equally important, islamophobic ideology served to justify permanent war in South Asia and the Middle East and the exorbitant military budgets, at a time of sharply deteriorating domestic socio-economic conditions. Hundreds of billions of dollars were spent unproductively as "Homeland Security" which strived in every way to recruit, train, frame and arrest Afro-American Muslim men as "terrorists". Thousands of secret agencies with hundreds of thousands of national, state and local officials spied on US citizens who at some point may have sought to speak or act to rectify or reform the militarist-financial-Zionist centered imperialist policies.

By the end of the first decade of the 21st century, the US empire could only destroy adversaries (Iraq, Pakistan, and Afghanistan), provoke military tensions (Korean peninsula, China Sea), and undermine relations with potentially lucrative trading partners (Iran, Venezuela). Galloping authoritarianism fused with fifth column Zionist militarism to foment islamophobic ideology. The convergence of authoritarian mediocrities, upwardly mobile knaves and fifth column tribal loyalists in the Obama regime precluded any foreseeable reversal of imperial decay.

China's growing global economic network and dynamic advance in cutting edge applied technology in everything from alternative energy to high speed trains, stands in contrast to the Zionist-militarist-infested empire of the US.

The US demands on client Pakistani rulers to empty their treasury in support of US colonial wars mainly against Islamic forces in Afghanistan and Pakistan, stands in contrast to the $30 billion dollar Chinese investments in infrastructure, energy and electrical power and multi-billion dollar increases in trade.

US $3 billion dollar military subsidies to Israel stand in contrast to China's multi-billion dollar investments in Iranian oil and trade agreements. US funding of wars against Islamic countries in Central and South Asia stands in contrast to Turkey's expanding economic trade and investment agreements in the same region. China has replaced the US as the key trading partner in leading South American countries, while the US unequal "free trade" agreement (NAFTA) impoverishes Mexico. Trade between the European Union and China exceeds that with the US.

In Africa, the US subsidizes wars in Somalia and the Horn of Africa, while China signs on to multi-billion dollar investment and trade agreements, building up African infrastructure in exchange for access to raw materials. There is no question that the economic future of Africa is increasingly linked to China unless disrupted by US intervention via Africom or Anglo-French intervention as in the Ivory Coast

The US Empire, in contrast, is locked in a deadly embrace with the 4th ranked military power (Israel) with a cutting edge in military technology, a puny market and universally hated colonial reputation. The US is tied to failed states in Yemen and Somalia, corrupt stagnant client regimes in Jordan, Egypt and the decadent rent collecting absolutist petrol-states of Saudi Arabia and the Gulf. All form part of an unproductive atavistic coalition bent on retaining power via military supremacy. Yet empires of the 21st century are built on the bases of productive economies with global networks linked to dynamic trading partners.

Recognizing the economic primacy and market opportunities linked to becoming part of the Chinese global network, former or existing US clients and even puppet rulers have begun to edge away from submission to US mandates. Fundamental shifts in economic relations and political alignments have occurred throughout Latin America. Brazil, Venezuela, Bolivia and other countries support Iran's non-military nuclear program in defiance of Zionist-led Washington aggression. Several countries have defied Israel-US policymakers by recognizing Palestine as a state. Trade with China surpasses trade with the US in the biggest countries in the region.

Puppet regimes in Iraq, Afghanistan and Pakistan have signed major economic agreements with China, Iran and Turkey even while the US pours billions to bolster its military position. Turkey, an erstwhile military client of the US-NATO command, broadens its ties with Iran, Central Asia and the Arab-Muslim world, challenging US-Israeli military hegemony.

The US Empire still retains major clients and nearly a thousand military bases around the world. As client and puppet regimes decline, Washington increases the role and scope of extra-territorial death squad operations from 50 to 80 countries. The growing independence of regimes in the developing world is especially fueled by an economic calculus: China offers greater economic returns and less political-military interference than the US.

Washington's imperial network is increasingly based on military ties with *allies:* Australia, Japan, South Korea, Taiwan in the Far East and Oceana; the European Union in the West; and a smattering of Central and South American states in the South. Even here, the military allies are no longer economic dependencies: Australia and New Zealand's principal export markets are in Asia (China). EU-China trade is growing exponentially. Japan, South Korea and Taiwan are increasingly tied by trade and investment with China ... as is Pakistan and India.

Equally important new regional networks which exclude the US are growing in Latin America and Asia, creating the potential for new economic blocs.

In other words the US imperial economic network constructed after World War II and amplified by the collapse of the USSR is in the process of decay, even as the military bases and treaties remain as a formidable 'platform' for new military interventions. The process of decay of the US Empire is both cause and consequence of the challenge by rising economic powers establishing alternative centers of growth and development. Changes within countries at the periphery of the empire and growing indebtedness and trade deficits at the 'center' of the empire are eroding the empire. The existing US governing class, in both its financial and militarist variants show neither will nor interest in confronting the causes of decay. Instead each mutually supports the other: the financial sector lowers taxes deepening the public debt and plunders the treasury. The military caste drains the treasury in pursuit of wars and military outposts and increases the trade deficit by undermining commercial and investment undertakings.

What is clear is that the military, political and ideological gains in network-building by the US around the world with the collapse of the USSR and the post-Soviet wars are not sustainable. On the contrary the overdevelopment of the ideological-military-security apparatus raised economic expectations and depleted economic resources resulting in the incapacity to exploit economic opportunities or consolidate economic networks. US funded "popular uprisings" in the Ukraine led to client regimes incapable of promoting growth. In the case of Georgia, the regime engaged in an adventurous war with Russia resulting in trade and territorial losses. It is a matter of time before existing client regimes in the Philippines and Mexico will face major upheavals, due to the precarious bases of rule by corrupt, stagnant and repressive rulers.

Perhaps most importantly, the upheavals in the Middle East have now begun, opening the opportunity for a decisive rupture with the current imperial-centered world economy and moving toward a social as well as political revolution.

NATO'S WAR CRIMES IN LIBYA

WHO GRIEVES FOR THE
FALLEN HEROES?

The conquest and occupation of Libya is first and foremost a military victory for NATO. Every aspect of the military offensive was spearheaded and directed by NATO air, sea and ground forces. The NATO invasion of Libya was basically a response to the "Arab spring": the popular uprisings which spread from North Africa to the Persian Gulf. The NATO assault formed part of a general counterattack designed to contain and reverse the popular democratic and anti-imperialist movements which had ousted or were on the verge of overthrowing US-client dictators.

Political and military considerations were foremost in motivating the NATO invasion: As late as May 2009, the U.S. and European regimes were developing close bilateral military, economic and security agreements with the Gaddafi regime. According the British daily, the *Independent*,[1] official Libyan documents found in its Foreign Office described how on December 16, 2003, the US CIA and British MI6 established close collaboration with the Gaddafi government. The MI6 provided Gaddafi with details on Libyan opposition leaders exiled in England and even drafted a speech for him as he sought rapprochement with the outside world.

U.S. Secretary of State Clinton presented Mutassin Gaddafi to the Washington press during a visit in 2009 stating, "*I am very pleased to welcome Minister Gaddafi to the State*

Department. We deeply value the relationship between the United States and Libya. We have many opportunities to deepen and broaden our co-operation and I am very much looking forward to building on this relationship."[2]

Between 2004-2010 the largest oil and petroleum service multinational corporations, including British Petroleum, Exxon Mobil, Halliburton, Chevron, Conoco and Marathon Oil joined with military-industrial giants like Raytheon and Northrop Grumman, Dow Chemical and Fluor to sign enormous investments and sales deals with Libya.[3]

General Dynamics signed a $165 million dollar deal in 2008 to equip Libya's elite mechanized brigade.[4] In 2009, the U.S. State Department awarded a $1.5 million dollar grant to train Libyan civilian and government security forces. The White House budget for 2012 included a grant for training Libyan security forces.

On August 24, 2011 Wikileaks released US embassy cables from Tripoli, which described the positive assessment a group of leading Republican senators had made of US-Libyan relations in during their visit in late 2009. These cables highlighted ongoing security training programs involving Gaddafi's police and military, as well as the US' strong support for the regime's repression of radical Islamists, many of whom are now leading the NATO-backed 'rebel forces' now occupying Tripoli.

What caused the NATO countries to *shift* abruptly from a policy of embracing Gaddafi to launching a brutal scorched-earth invasion of Libya in a matter of months? The key is the popular uprisings, which threatened Euro-US domination. The near total destruction of Libya, a secular regime with the highest standard of living in Africa, was meant to be a lesson, a message from the imperialists to the newly aroused masses of North Africa, Asia and Latin America: *The fate of Libya awaits any regime which aspires to greater independence and questions the ascendancy of Euro-American power.*

NATO's savage six-month blitz—over 30,000 air and missile assaults on Libyan civil and military institutions—

was a response to those who claimed that the US and the EU were on the "decline" and that the "empire was in decay". The radical Islamist and monarchist-led "uprising" in Benghazi during March 2011 was backed by and served as a pretext for the NATO imperial powers to extend their counter-offensive on the road to *neo-colonial restoration*.

NATO's War and the Phony "Rebel Uprising"

Nothing is more obvious than the fact that the entire war against Libya was in every strategic and material fashion NATO's war. The casting of the rag-tag collection of monarchists, Islamist fundamentalists, London and Washington-based ex-pats and disaffected Gaddafi officials as "rebels" is a pure case of mass media propaganda. From the beginning the 'rebels' depended completely on the military, political, diplomatic and media power of NATO, without which the *de facto* mercenaries would not have lasted a month, holed up in Benghazi.

A detailed analysis of the main features of the conquest of Libya confirms this assault as a *NATO war.*

NATO launched brutal air and sea attacks destroying the Libyan air force, ships, energy depots, tanks, artillery and armories, and killed and wounded thousands of soldiers, police and civilian militia fighters. Until NATO's invasion the mercenary 'rebel' ground forces had not advanced beyond Benghazi and could barely 'hold' territory afterwards. The 'rebel' mercenaries 'advanced' only behind the withering round-the-clock air attacks of the NATO offensive.

NATO air strikes were responsible for the massive destruction of Libyan civilian and defensive military infrastructure, bombing ports, highways, warehouses, airports, hospitals, electrical and water plants and neighborhood housing in a war of 'terror' designed to 'turn' the loyalist mass base against the Gaddafi government. The mercenaries did not have popular backing among Libyan civilians, but NATO brutality weakened active opposition against the 'rebel' mercenaries.

NATO won key diplomatic support for the invasion by securing UN resolutions, mobilizing their client rulers in the Arab League, procuring US mercenary trained 'legionnaires' from Qatar and the financial backing of the rich rabble in the Gulf. NATO forced 'cohesion' among the feuding clans of self-appointed 'rebel' mercenary leaders via its seizure ("freezing") of Libyan government overseas assets amounting to billions of dollars. Thus the financing, arming, training and advising by "Special Forces" were all under NATO control.

NATO imposed economic sanctions, cutting off Libya's income from oil sales. NATO ran an intensive propaganda campaign, parading the imperial offensive as a "rebel uprising"; disguising the blistering bombardment of a defenseless anti-colonial army as 'humanitarian intervention' in defense of 'pro-democracy civilians'. The centrally choreographed mass media blitz extended far beyond the usual liberal circles to convince 'progressive' journalists and their newspapers, as well as intellectuals to paint the imperial mercenaries as 'rebels' and to condemn the heroic 6-month resistance of the Libyan army and people against foreign aggression.

The pathologically racist Euro-US propaganda published lurid images of Libyan government troops (often portrayed as 'black mercenaries') receiving massive quantities of 'Viagra' from Gaddafi while their own families and homes were, in fact, under aerial assault and blockade by NATO.

The main contribution of the mercenary 'conquerors' in this grand production was to provide photo opportunities of rag-tag 'rebels' waving rifles in Pentagon-style Che Guevara poses riding around in pickup trucks arresting and brutalizing African migrant workers and black Libyans. The mercenary 'liberators' triumphantly entered Libyan cities and towns, which were already scorched and devastated by the NATO colonial air force. Needless to say, the mass media 'adored' them.

In the aftermath of NATO's destruction, the 'rebel'

mercenaries showed their true talents as death squads: They organized the systematic execution of "suspected Gaddafi supporters" and the pillage of homes, stores, banks and public institutions related to the defeated regime. To "secure" Tripoli and snuff out any expression of anti-colonial resistance, the 'rebel' mercenaries carried out summary executions—especially of black Libyans and sub-Saharan African workers and their families. The "chaos" in Tripoli described by the mass media is due to the self-styled 'liberation' forces running amok. The only quasi-organized forces in Tripoli appear to be the Al Qaeda-linked militants, NATO's erstwhile allies.

Consequences of the NATO Conquest of Libya

According to 'rebel' mercenary technocrats, NATO's policy of systematic destruction will cost Libya at least a 'lost decade'. This is an optimistic assessment of how long 'reconstruction' will take for Libya to regain the economic levels of February 2011. The major petroleum companies have already lost hundreds of millions in profits and over the decade are expected to lose billions more due to the flight, assassination and jailing of thousands of experienced Libyan and foreign experts, skilled immigrant workers and technical specialists in all fields, especially in view of the destruction of Libyan infrastructure and telecommunication systems.

Sub-Sahara Africa will suffer a huge set-back with the cancellation of the proposed 'Bank of Africa', which Gaddafi was developing as an alternative source of investment finance and the destruction of his alternative communications system for Africa. The process of re-colonization involving imperial rule via NATO and UN mercenary 'peace keepers' will be chaotic, given the inevitable strife among hostile armed Islamist fundamentalists, monarchists, neo-colonial technocrats, tribal warlords and clans as they carve up their private fiefdoms. Intra-imperial rivalries and local political claimants to the oil wealth will further enhance the 'chaos' and degrade civilian life in a nation which had once boasted the highest per capita income and standard of living in Africa. Complex irrigation and petroleum networks, developed under Gaddafi and destroyed by NATO, will remain in shambles. As the example of Iraq has vividly proved, NATO is better at destroying than at constructing a modern secular state rooted in a modern civil bureaucracy, with universal free public education, a secular judicial system and modern health service—as enjoyed by Iraq before "shock and awe". The US policy of rule and ruin reigns supreme in NATO's juggernaut.

Motivation for the Invasion

What motivated NATO to initiate a massive, six-month long aerial bombardment of Libya, followed by invasion and crimes against humanity? Civilian deaths and the widespread destruction of Libyan civil society by NATO flies in the face of its claims that the air assaults were meant to "protect civilians" from imminent Gaddafi-led genocide—'rebel' claims which were never substantiated. The bombing of Libya's critical economic infrastructure allows us to categorically conclude that the NATO assault has little to do with 'economic rationality' or any such consideration. The primary motivation for NATO's actions can be found in earlier policies related to a spring *counteroffensive* against the mass popular movements that overthrew US-EU puppets in Egypt and Tunisia and were threatening client regimes in Yemen, Bahrain and elsewhere.

Despite the fact that the US-NATO were already engaged in several colonial wars (Iraq, Afghanistan, Pakistan, Yemen and Somalia) and Western public opinion had been demanding withdrawal in light of the costs, Western imperial leaders felt too much was at stake and calculated that losses could be minimized. NATO's overwhelming mastery of the air and sea made short work of Libya's puny military defense capability, allowing it to bomb the cities, ports and vital infrastructure with impunity and enforce a total economic blockade. NATO calculated that massive bombing would terrorize the Libyan people into submission and bring about a quick colonial victory without any NATO military losses— the prime concern of Western public opinion—and permit a triumphant 'rebel' mercenary army to march into Tripoli.

The Arab popular rebellions were the central concern and the motor force behind NATO's destruction of Libya. These mass popular uprisings had toppled the longstanding pillars of US-Israel-EU dominance in the Middle East. The fall of the Egyptian dictator Hosni Mubarak and his Tunisian counterpart, Ben Ali, sent tremors through the imperial foreign offices. These successful uprisings had the immediate ripple effect of inspiring similar movements throughout the region. Bahrain, housing the key naval base for the US navy in the Middle East and neighboring Saudi Arabia (the US key strategic ally in the Arab world), witnessed a prolonged massive uprising of civil society, while Yemen ruled by the US puppet, Ali Saleh, faced mass popular movements and militant resistance. Morocco and Algeria were experiencing popular demands for democracy. The common thread in the Arab peoples' movements was their demands to end EU, US and Israeli domination of the region, an end to massive corruption and nepotism, and for free elections and a solution to widespread unemployment via large-scale job programs. As anti-colonial movements grew in breadth and intensity their demands radicalized from political to social democracy, from a democratic to an anti-imperialist foreign policy. Workers' demands were enforced by strikes and calls for the prosecution of repressive police and internal security and of military officials guilty of crimes against their citizens.

The US, EU and Israel were caught by surprise—their intelligence agencies so deeply embedded in the smelly crevices of their clients' secret police institutions failed to detect the popular explosions. The popular uprisings came at a critical and inopportune moment, especially for the US where domestic support for NATO wars in Iraq and Afghanistan had declined sharply given the economic crises and major social cutbacks required to pay for these wars. Moreover, in Iraq and Afghanistan the US-NATO troops were losing ground: the Taliban was, in effect, the real 'shadow government'. Pakistan, despite its puppet regime and compliant generals, faced overwhelming popular opposition to the air war against its citizens in frontier villages and towns. The US drone strikes killing militants and civilians were answered with the sabotage of vital transport supplying the occupation forces in Afghanistan. Faced with the deteriorating global situation, the NATO powers, decided that they needed to counterattack in the most decisive and visible manner by destroying an independent, secular regime like Libya and thereby re-affirming their global supremacy, countering the image of defeat and retreat and, above all, re-energizing the "declining imperial power".

The Imperial Counterattack

The US led the way in its counter-offensive in Egypt, by backing the power grab by the military junta led by Mubarak loyalists, who then proceeded to disperse and repress the pro-democracy and workers' movements and to end all talk of restructuring the economy. A pro-NATO collective dictatorship of generals replaced the personal autocratic rule of Hosni Mubarak. The NATO powers provided "emergency" billions to float the new regime and 'derail' the Egyptian people's march to democracy. In Tunisia a similar process took hold: the EU, especially France and the US, backed a reshuffling of the ousted regime, bringing to the fore a new/old cast of neo-colonial politicians. They plied them with funds, insuring that the military-police apparatus remained intact despite continued mass discontent with the conformist policies of the 'new/old regime.

In Bahrain and Yemen, the NATO powers followed a dual track, unsure of the outcome between the massive pro-democracy movements and the pro-imperial autocrats. In Bahrain, the West called for 'reform' and 'dialogue' with the majority Shia population and a peaceful resolution, while continuing to arm and protect the Bahraini royalty— all the while looking for a pliant alternative if the incumbent puppet was overthrown. The NATO-backed Saudi invasion of Bahrain in support of the dictatorship and the subsequent wave of terror effectively showed West's true intentions. In Yemen the NATO powers continued to support the brutal Ali Saleh regime.

Meanwhile the NATO powers were exploiting internal discontent in Syria by arming and providing diplomatic support to the Islamic fundamentalists and their minority neo-liberal allies in an effort to overthrow the Bashar al-Assad regime. Thousands of Syrian civilians, police and soldiers have been killed in this simmering civil war, which NATO propaganda presents as a case of state terror against 'peaceful civilians', ignoring the killing of soldiers and civilians by armed Islamists and the very real threat to Syria's secular population and religious minorities.

The Counter-Offensive and NATO's Invasion of Libya

The destruction and invasion of Libya reversed seven years of accommodation and co-operation with Gaddafi. There were no 'incidents' in Libya or elsewhere that had threatened the NATO countries' economic and military interests. Libya was still an independent country, pursuing a pro-African agenda which had spearheaded and funded the establishment of an independent regional bank and communications system designed to bypass IMF and World Bank control. Libya's close ties to all the major NATO oil companies and to Wall Street investment banks as well as its ongoing bilateral military programs with the US did not shield it from the NATO's attack. Libya was deliberately destroyed by a 6-month campaign of relentless bombing by NATO air and naval forces to serve as an *example* to the Arab popular movements: NATO's message to the Arab pro-democracy movements was that it was prepared to launch new offensive wars with the same devastating consequences as the Libyan people had just endured; that the imperial powers were not in decline and any independent anti-colonial regime would suffer the same fate. NATO's message to the African Union was clear: There will be no independent regional bank organized by Gaddafi or anyone else. There is no alternative to imperial banks, the IMF or the World Bank.

Through the devastation of Libya, the West was telling the Third World that, contrary to the pundits who chattered about 'the decline of the US empire', NATO was willing to use overwhelming and genocidal military power to establish puppet regimes, no matter how backward, vicious and regressive the puppets, because they will ultimately obey NATO and answer to the White House.

NATO's invasion and destruction of a secular modern republic like Libya, which had used its oil wealth to develop Libyan society, was a stern message to democratic popular movements. Any independent Third World regime can be rolled back; colonial puppet regimes can be foisted onto a devastated people; the end of colonialism is *not* inevitable, imperial rule is back.

NATO's invasion of Libya sends a message to freedom fighters everywhere: There is a high cost to independence; acting outside of imperial channels, even if only to a limited degree, can bring swift destruction. Moreover, the NATO war on Libya demonstrates to all nationalist regimes that *making concessions* to Western economic, political and military interests—as Gaddafi's sons and their neoliberal entourage had done, pursuing full accommodation—does not offer security. In fact concessions may have *encouraged* imperial penetration. The West's burgeoning ties with Libyan officials facilitated their defections and promised an easy victory over Tripoli. The NATO powers believed that with a regional uprising in Benghazi, a handful of defectors from the Gaddafi regime and their military control of the air and sea, Libya would be an easy victory on the way to a widespread *rollback of the Arab Spring*.

The "cover" of an orchestrated regional military-civilian "uprising" and the imperial mass media propaganda blitz against the Libyan government was sufficient to convince the majority of western leftist intellectuals to take up the cudgels for the mercenary 'rebels": Samir Amin, Immanuel Wallerstein, Michel Lowy, Juan Cole and many others backed the mercenary "rebels" ... demonstrating the irrelevance and bankruptcy of the remnants of the old left.

The Long Term, Large Scale Consequences of NATO's War

The invasion and conquest of Libya marks a new phase in Western imperialism's drive to reassert its primacy in the Arab-Islamic world. The ongoing offensive is clearly evident in the mounting pressures, sanctions, and arming of the Syrian opposition to Bashar al-Assad, the ongoing consolidation of the Egyptian military junta and the demobilization of the pro-democracy movement in Tunisia. How far "backwards" the process can be pushed depends on the revitalization and regrouping of the pro-democracy movements, currently in ebb.

Unfortunately, NATO's victory over Libya will strengthen the arguments of the militarist wings of the US and EU ruling class who claim that the 'military option' brings results, that the only policy that "the anti-colonial Arabs" understand is force. The Libyan outcome will strengthen the hand of policymakers who favor a continued long-term US-NATO presence in Iraq and Afghanistan and promote a military offensive against Iran and Syria. Israel has already capitalized on NATO's victory against Gaddafi via its expansion of huge colonial settlements in the West Bank, increasing bombing and missile raids on Gaza, plus a major naval and army build-up in the Red Sea region adjoining Egypt and confrontational posturing toward Turkey.

On September 20, 2011, the African Union, recognized the mercenary "transition" regime imposed by NATO on Libya. Aside from the Libyan people, Sub-

Saharan Africa will be the biggest immediate loser in the overthrow of Gaddafi. Libya's generous aid, grants and loans, bought the African states a degree of independence from the harsh conditions of the IMF, World Bank and Western bankers. Gaddafi was a major sponsor and backer of regional integration—including the African Union. His large scale development programs, especially oil and water infrastructure and construction projects, employed hundreds of thousands of sub-Saharan African immigrant workers and specialists who remitted billions to their home countries, helping the balance of payments and reducing deficits and poverty at home. In place of Gaddafi's positive *economic* contribution, Africa now faces Tripoli transformed into a colonial outpost, fortifying US military command in Africa and a new push to strengthen military ties within the empire.

However, beyond the present-day celebrations of their imperial military success in Libya, the war only exacerbates the weakening of Western economies by diverting scarce domestic resources to wage prolonged wars with no decisive victories assuring stability and economic reward. Ongoing social cuts and harsh austerity programs have undercut any ruling class efforts to whip up phony mass chauvinist celebrations for "democratic victories over tyrants". The naked aggression against Libya has heightened Russian, Chinese and Venezuelan security concerns. Russia and China will veto any UN Security Council sanctions on Syria. Venezuela and Russia are signing new multi-billion dollar military co-operation agreements, strengthening Caracas's military defense in the wake of the Libyan invasion.

For all the ruling class and mass media euphoria, the 'win' over Libya, grotesque and criminal in the destruction of Libyan secular society and the ongoing brutalization of black Libyans, does not solve the profound economic crises in the EU-US. It does not affect China's growing competitive advantages over its western competitors. It does not end US-Israeli isolation faced with an imminent worldwide recognition of Palestine as an independent state, following its acceptance by UNESCO as a member state. The absence of left-wing western intellectual solidarity for independent Third World nations, evident in their support for the imperial-based mercenary "rebels," is more than compensated by the emergence of a radical new generation of left-wing activists in South Africa, Chile, Greece, Spain, Egypt, Pakistan and elsewhere. These are youth whose solidarity with anti-colonial regimes is based on their own experience of exploitation, "marginalization" (unemployment) and repression at home.

Is it too much to hope that a War Crimes Tribunal could be organized to prosecute NATO leaders for crimes against humanity, for genocide against the people of Libya? Can the brutal link between costly imperial wars abroad and increasing austerity and domestic decay lead to the revival of an anti-imperialist peace movement based on withdrawal of imperial troops abroad and public domestic investments for jobs, health and education for the working and middle class?

If the destruction and occupation of Libya marks a time of infamy for the NATO powers, it also establishes a new awareness that a people can struggle and resist 6 months of intense, massive bombings from all the NATO powers. Perhaps when their heroic example becomes clear and the fog of media propaganda is lifted, a new emerging generation of fighters will vindicate the assault on Libya, continuing the struggle for the definitive emancipation of the Afro-Arab and Islamic peoples from the yoke of Western imperialism.

ENDNOTES

1   *The Independent*, 9/4/2011.
2   examiner.com, 2/26/2011.
3   Ibid.
4   Ibid.

THE ASSASSINATION OF OSAMA BIN LADEN

ITS USE AND ABUSE

The assassination of bin Laden has been celebrated as a great strategic victory by the White House, the European capitals and all the major mass media outlets throughout the world. The killing has served as a major propaganda tool to enhance the standing of the US military in the eyes of the domestic public and to serve as a warning to overseas adversaries.

Contrary to this immense propaganda campaign and despite whatever *symbolic* value the killing may have in the eyes of his executioners—and bearing in mind that there are many who question whether it even occurred at all—there is no evidence that the death will have any impact on the deteriorating military and political position of the US in South Asia, the Middle East, North Africa or elsewhere.

Bin Laden and Al Qaeda

Even in terms of weakening, let alone defeating Al Qaeda, the killing will have minimal effect. Al Qaeda is a highly *decentralized* organization, a loose collection of groups distributed throughout the conflict zones, each with its own leaders, programs, tactics and strategies. Al Qaeda is not a centralized international organization dependent on a 'central command' directed by a single person: bin Laden was an ideological symbol more than an operative leader directing operations. His death merely led to the appointment of Dr. Ayman al-Zawahiri, al Qaeda's theological leader, as its new leader and will have zero impact on the rest of the loosely associated global network of groups which call themselves Al Qaeda. Hence, whatever actions and activities entities called Al Qaeda have taken in the past will continue into the future.

Bin Laden and the Afghan Resistance

The killing of bin Laden will have the most minimum impact in Afghanistan, for the obvious reason that the major forces carrying out the armed resistance there are the Taliban and various other independent nationalist movements. The Taliban is *totally independent* of Al Qaeda in its origins, structure, leadership, tactics, strategy and social composition. Moreover, the Taliban is a mass organization with roots and sympathizers throughout the country. It has tens of thousands of trained Afghans fighters; it has deeply penetrated the Afghani government and military and on May 1, 2011 announced a major 'spring offensive'. The Taliban is overwhelmingly 'national' in it composition, leadership and ideology, while Al Qaeda is 'international' (Arab) in its membership and leadership. The Taliban may have tolerated or even in certain circumstances tactically collaborated with Al Qaeda, but at no point is there any evidence that it took orders from bin Laden. The overwhelming majority of US and NATO casualties in Afghanistan were inflicted by the Taliban. The major bases of operation and support in Pakistan are linked to the Taliban. In summary the killing of Osama bin Laden will have zero impact on the correlation of forces in Afghanistan; it will have zero impact on the capacity of the Taliban to carry-out its prolonged war against the US occupation and inflict dozens of casualties each week.

Bin Laden and the Mass Arab Revolts

From Tunisia to the Gulf States, mass popular revolts

have either overthrown US collaborator regimes or are on the verge of doing so. Al Qaeda had played a *minor* role, except perhaps among the Libyan "rebels". In Egypt and Tunisia, the mass movements embracing a wide gamut of secular students, trade unions and civic groups and moderate Islamic movements have dominated the uprisings. Al Qaeda is a marginal factor and bin Laden is a very marginal figure, where he is not openly rejected. The killing of bin Laden will not have any impact on the rising anti-imperialist sentiments which inform these mass movements. Some commentators even suggest that the killing will weaken White House propaganda efforts to justify US military operations under the pretext of "anti-terrorist" activities.

Bin Laden and Iraq/Iran

The major opposition to the US in Iraq is the Shia majority, minority Sunnis and ex-Ba'athists. In short, just about everybody. Al Qaeda's terrorist actions have played a minor role and do not resonate with the mass of Iraqis demanding a US withdrawal. The major religious based mass anti-occupation movements have their own leaders and militias and community bases; none accept Al Qaeda leadership or even collaboration. Al Qaeda in Iraq played a divisive role, attacking Shia (inter alia killing at least 86 including Ayatollah Sayed Mohammed Baqir al-Hakim in the Imam Ali Mosque bombing in Najaf), Iraqi civilians ((including the October 2004 ambush and massacre of 49 unarmed Iraqi National Guard recruits) and internationals (including the chief of the United Nations mission to Iraq). The US withdrawal is a response to mass pressure from below, it is not a result of civilian deaths from the occasional Al Qaeda "suicide bombers"—or even their audacious suicide bombings of the high security Green Zone. Clearly the retreat of the US from Iraq was not affected by the killing of bin Laden but rather by the refusal of the US-installed Maliki government, swayed by overwhelming popular pressure, to provide immunity for any remaining US soldiers. Nor will the transition be affected by his local followers.

Bin Laden and Iran

The Iranian Islamic regime was a mortal enemy of Al Qaeda, jailing suspects and early in the Afghan war (2001-2003) collaborating with the US in its pursuit of its followers. Both strands of the political opposition, secular and religious, were hostile to Al Qaeda, in view of its anti-Shia orientation. As a result, bin Laden had very little organized influence, even as he may have had a mass appeal as a symbol of armed resistance to the US: "The enemy of our enemy is our friend". The killing of bin Laden will not have any impact on Iran which has its own icon "Khomeini"; its own brand of Islamic nationalism and is much more engaged in supporting Syria, Hezbollah and Hamas. The US will not gain the least advantage in its efforts to undermine or destroy its Iranian adversaries.

The Significance of the bin Laden Assassination

Clearly the killing of bin Laden has absolutely no strategic or tactical importance in the major theaters of war and political revolt in the Arab world.

The major significance of the killing is in the context of the strategic military and political defeats suffered by the US, especially most recently in Afghanistan. On April 27, 2011, nine senior US military officers were assassinated by a "trusted" Afghan fighter pilot in the high security Kabul airport. Four majors, two captains and two lieutenant colonials were killed in the single biggest killing of high US military officials in the 20th and 21st century wars. Several facts mark this out as a strategically important event. It took place in a high security installation, suggesting that *no place* in Afghanistan is safe from deadly armed attacks by the Taliban or the armed resistance. This means that all US military, no matter how high their rank, are vulnerable to deadly attack. Furthermore, no US trained Afghan military official or soldier can be considered "loyal"—even those most closely in collaboration can and *will* turn their guns on their "mentors".

If the US cannot protect its senior officers in its highest security compounds, how can it claim to have "secured" any of the territory outside—namely the cities, towns and villages? Two weeks earlier, with the collaboration of jail officials, almost 500 jailed Taliban fighters and leaders escaped via a 300 meter tunnel to a dozen waiting trucks. Only two years earlier 900 prisoners also escaped. In its aftermath the US insisted on the appointment of "highly screened" loyalist collaborators as heads and directors of security and prisons, to no avail.

The overwhelming evidence shows that the US war effort is failing to create an effective puppet regime in Afghanistan. The Taliban is slowly but surely eroding US influence. In the face of major strategic losses, as evident in the astonishing assassination of top military officials, Obama had to mount a political spectacle—a "military success story"—the killing of an unarmed bin Laden, to buoy the spirits of the American public, military and its NATO followers. While the event might have provided an opportunity for the US to exit from Afghanistan, claiming "mission accomplished"—it did not do so, and is more likely to leave ignominiously. Every popular uprising against US puppets in North Africa and the Middle East is a political defeat—it is not too much to expect that even the appearance of success in Libya will soon disintegrate, as by December, 2011 thousands were marching in Tripoli, some twenty thousand in the former "rebel stronghold" of Ben Ghazi, demanding democracy and an end to the secrecy of the new regime.[1] The enduring regime in Iran is a defeat for the US-Israel bellicose efforts for regime change. So Obama and his mass media acolytes have to mega magnify the killing of an isolated, political leader of a loose association of marginal terrorists as a world shattering, game turning event, when in fact, the losses and defeats accumulate every day before, during and after the assassination.

The Taliban didn't even blink – their 'spring offensive' marched on; US military officials remain wary of any encounters with any 'loyal' Afghan collaborators. Egypt rejects US-Israeli politics toward the unity of Palestinians; the revolts in the Gulf continue. And the fighting in Libya has not ended—it may have only begun...

ENDNOTES

1   Chris Stephens, "Libyans March in Tripoli, Benghazi, Calling for Less Secrecy From Leaders", *Bloomberg*, December 13, 2011.

THE ASSASSINATION OF ANWAR AL-AWLAKI BY FIAT

"What was a science-fiction scenario not much more than a decade agohas become today's news. In Iraq and Afghanistan, military drones have become a routine part of the arsenal. In Pakistan, according to American officials, strikes from Predators and Reapers operated by the *C.I.A.* have killed more than 2,000 militants; the number of civilian casualties is hotly debated. In Yemen last month, an American citizen was, for the first time, the intended target of a drone strike, as Anwar al-Awlaki, **the Qaeda propagandist** and plotter, was killed along with a second American, Samir Khan."

The New York Times[1]

"The secret document provided the justification for acting despite an executive order banning assassinations, a federal law against murder, protections in the Bill of Rights and various strictures of the international laws of war, according to people familiar with the analysis."

The New York Times[2]

The Assassination of Anwar Al-Awlaki by Fiat

The killing of Anwar al-Awlaki, a U.S citizen in Yemen, by a CIA drone missile on September 30, 2011 has been publicized by the mass media, President Obama, and the usual experts on al-Qaeda as "a major blow to the jihadist network founded by Osama bin Laden". US officials called Awlaki "the most dangerous figure in Al-Qaeda".[3]

There is ample evidence to suggest that the publicity surrounding the killing of al-Awlaki has greatly exaggerated his political importance and is an attempt to cover up the declining influence of the US in the Islamic world. The State Department's declaration of a major victory serves to exaggerate US military capacity to defeat its adversaries. The assassination serves to justify Obama's arbitrary use of death squads to execute US critics and adversaries overseas by executive fiat, denying the accused the most elementary judicial protections.

Myths About al-Awlaki

Al-Awlaki was a theological blogger in a small, poor Islamic country (Yemen). His efforts were confined to propagandizing against Western countries, attempting to influence Islamic believers to resist Western military and cultural intervention. Within Yemen, his organizational affiliations were with a minority sector of the mass popular opposition to US-backed dictator Ali Abdullah Saleh. His fundamentalist group was largely influential in a few small towns in southern Yemen. He was *not a military or political leader* in his organization, dubbed by the West as "Al-Qaeda in the Arabian Peninsula" (AQAP). Like most of what the CIA calls "Al-Qaeda", AQAP was a local autonomous organization, meaning that it was organized and controlled by local leaders even as it expressed agreement with many other loosely associated fundamentalist groups. Awlaki had a very limited role in the Yemeni groups' military and political operations and virtually no influence in the mass movement engaged in ousting Saleh. There is *no evidence*, documented or observable, that he was "a very effective propagandist" as ex-CIA and now Brookings Institution member Bruce Riedal claims. In Yemen and among the mass popular movements in Tunisia, Egypt, Bahrain and elsewhere his followers were few and far between. One "expert" cites such intangibles as his "spiritual leadership", which is as good a way as any to avoid the test of empirical evidence: apparently a crystal ball or a tarot reading will do.

Given the paucity of evidence demonstrating Awlaki's political and ideological influence among the mass movements in North Africa, the Middle East or Asia, the US intelligence agencies claim his "real influence was among English-speaking jihadi, some of whom he groomed personally to carry out attacks on the US."

In other words Washington's casting Awlaki as an "important threat" revolves around his speeches and writings, since he had *no operational role* in organizing suicide bomb attacks—or at least no concrete evidence has been presented of same to date.

The intelligence agencies "suspect" he was involved in the plot that dispatched bombs in cargo aircraft from Yemen to Chicago in October 2010. US intelligence claims he provided a "theological justification" via e-mail for US army Major Nidal Malik's killing of 13 people at Fort Hood. In other words, like many US philosophical writers and legal experts such as Princeton's Michael Walzer and Harvard's Alan Dershowitz, Awlaki discussed "just wars" and the "right" of violent action. If political writings and speeches of publicists are cited by an assassin as the basis for their action, should the White House execute leading US Islamophobes like Marilyn Geller and Daniel Pipes, cited as his inspiration by Norwegian mass murderer Anders Behring Brevik? Or does their Zionist affiliation provide them immunity from Navy Seal assaults and drone missiles?

Even assuming that the unsubstantiated "suspicions" of the CIA, MI 16 and the Al Qaeda "experts" are correct and Awlaki had a direct or indirect hand in "terrorist action" against the US, these activities were absurdly amateurish and abject failures, certainly not a serious threat to our security. The "underwear bomber" Umar Farouk Abdul

Mutallab's effort to ignite bomb materials on a flight to Detroit, December 25, 2009, led to roasting his testicles! Likewise the bombs dispatched in cargo aircraft from Yemen to Chicago in October 2010 were another bungled job.

If anything, the Yemenite AQAP's hopeless, hapless operational planning served to highlight its technical incompetence. In fact according to Mutallab's own admission, published on NBC news at the time, Awlaki played no role in the planning or execution of the bomb attack. He merely served to refer Mutallab to the Al Qaeda organization.

Clearly, Awlaki was a minor figure in Yemen's political struggles. He was a propagandist of little influence in the mass movements during the "Arab Spring". He was an inept recruiter of English-speaking would be bombers. The claims that he planned and "hatched" two bomb plots[4] are refuted by the confession of one bomber and the absence of any corroboratory evidence regarding the failed cargo bombs.

The mass media inflate the importance of Awlaki to the stature of a major al-Qaeda leader and subsequently, his killing as a "major psychological blow" to worldwide jihadists. This imagery has no substance. But the puff pieces do have a very important propaganda purpose. Worse still, the killing of Awlaki provides a justification for extra-judicial serial state assassinations of ideological critics of Anglo-American leaders engaged in bloody colonial wars.

Propaganda to Bolster Flagging Military Morale

Recent events strongly suggest that the US and its NATO allies are losing the war in Afghanistan to the Taliban: top collaborator officials are knocked off at the drop of a Taliban turban. After years of occupation, Iraq is moving closer to Iran rather than to the US. Libya in the post-Gaddafi period is under warring mercenary forces squaring off for a fight for the billion dollar booty. Al Qaeda prepares battle against the neoliberal expats and Gaddafi renegades.

Washington and NATO's attempt to regain the

initiative via puppet rulers in Egypt, Tunisia, Bahrain and Yemen is being countered by a "second wave" of mass pro-democracy movements. The "Arab Spring" is being followed by a "hot autumn". Positive news and favorable outcomes for Obama are few and far between. He has run out of any pseudo-populist initiative to enchant the Arab-Islamic masses. His rhetoric rings hollow in the face of his UN speech denying recognition to an independent Palestinian state. His groveling before Israel is clearly seen as an effort to bolster his re-election campaign financing by wealthy Zionists.

Diplomatically isolated and domestically in trouble over failed economic policies, Obama pulls the trigger and shoots an itinerant Muslim preacher in Yemen to send a "message" to the Arab world. In a word he says, "If you, the Arabs, the Islamic world, won't join us, we can and will execute those of you who can be labeled "spiritual mentors" or are suspected of harboring terrorists."

Obama's defense of *systematic* killing of ideological critics, denying US constitutional norms of judicial due process to a U.S citizen and in blatant rejection of international law defines a homicidal executive.

Let us be absolutely clear what the larger implications are of political murder by executive fiat. If the President can order the murder of a dual American-Yemeni citizen abroad on the basis of his ideological-theological beliefs, what is to stop him from ordering the same in the US? If he uses arbitrary violence to compensate for diplomatic failure abroad, what is to stop him from declaring a "heightened internal security threat" in order to suspend our remaining freedoms at home and to round up critics?

We seriously understate our "Obama problem" if we think of this ordered killing merely as an isolated murder of a "jihadist" in strife torn Yemen … Obama's murder of Awlaki has profound, long term significance because it *puts political assassinations at the center of US foreign and domestic policy*. As Secretary of Defense Panetta states, "eliminating home grown terrorists" is at the core of our "internal security".

ENDNOTES

1. Scott Shane, "Coming Soon: The Drone Arms Race", *The New York Times*, October 8, 2011
2. "Secret U.S. Memo Made Legal Case to Kill a Citizen," *The New York* Times, Saturday, October 9, 2011 at <http://www.nytimes.com/2011/10/09/world/middleeast/secret-us-memo-made-legal-case-to-kill-a-citizen.html?emc=na>
3. *Financial Times*, Oct. 1 and 2, 2011.
4. Ibid.

THE OBAMA DOCTRINE

MAKING A VIRTUE OF NECESSITY

After nearly 3 years in deep pursuit of the colonial wars initiated by ex-President Bush, the Obama regime has finally recognized the catastrophic domestic and foreign consequences. As a result the "reality principle" has taken hold; the maintenance of the US Empire requires modification of tactics and strategies, to cut political, military and diplomatic losses. In response to major military and political losses as well as new opportunity, the White House is fashioning a new doctrine of imperial conquest based on intensified aerial warfare, greater extra-territorial intervention and, when circumstances allow, alliances with collaborators. This includes the arming and financial backing of retrograde despotic regimes in the Gulf city-states, fundamentalists, opportunist defectors, mercenaries, academic exiles gangsters and other rabble willing to serve the empire for a price.

Whether these 'changes' add up to a new post-colonial "Obama doctrine" or simply reflects a series of improvisations resulting from past losses ("making a virtue of necessity" remains to be seen.

We will proceed by outlining the *strategic failures* which set the context for the "rethinking" of the Bush-Obama policies in mid- 2011. We will then point out the 'reality principle"—the deep crises and rising pressures— which *forced* the Obama regime to modify its methods of imperial warfare. Obama's changes are designed to retain levers of power under conditions of limited resources and with dubious allies. The third section will describe these changes as they have occurred, emphasizing their reactive nature—improvised—as unfavorable circumstances evolve and favorable opportunities arose. The final section will critically evaluate Obama's new imperial policies, their impact on targeted countries and peoples as well as the consequences for the US.

The Bush-Obama Continuum 2009-2011

Obama took his lead from the Bush administration and ran with it. He expanded war budgets to over $750 billion; increased ground troops by 30,000 in Afghanistan; expanded expenditures on base building and mercenary troop recruitment in Iraq; multiplied US air and ground incursions in Yemen, Pakistan, Somalia, and, albeit via NATO, Libya. As a result the budget deficit reached $1.6 trillion; the trade deficit reached unsustainable levels and the recession deepened. Public support for Obama and the Democrats plummeted. Parallel to Obama's skyrocketing external imperial expenditures, he spent hundreds of billions of dollars in dozens of internal security agencies, further depleting the treasury. Greater debts abroad and deficits at home were accompanied by the trillion dollar bailout of Wall Street while 10 million homes were foreclosed and unemployment reached double digits.

Obama retained and expanded the Bush era wars, bailouts, and millionaire tax exemptions and proposed draconian cuts in social security, federally-funded medical programs and education. Despite massive military commitments, Obama could not secure a single major military victory. By the beginning of the third year of his regime, it was abundantly clear that amidst the wreckage of the domestic economy and the demise of key overseas collaborator regimes, the US Empire was under siege.

The Reality Principle

The reality of massive expenditures in losing wars and faltering support at home and abroad finally penetrated the thinking of even the most dogmatic and intransigent militarist ideologues in the Obama regime. Nationalist Islamists were a "shadow" government throughout Afghanistan, inflicting increasing casualties on US-NATO forces even in the capital, Kabul. In Iraq even the puppet regime rejected a minimum US military presence, as warring factions sharpened their knives, preparing for a post-colonial showdown between willing colonial collaborators, resistance fighters, sects, tribes, death squads, ethnic separatists and mercenaries. Despite US military threats and Zionist designed economic sanctions, Iran gained influence throughout the region, eroding US influence in Iraq, Syria, western Afghanistan, the Gulf, Lebanon and Palestine (especially Gaza).

The fall of major US client regimes in Egypt and Tunisia (Mubarak and Ben Ali), and mass uprisings threatening other puppets in Yemen, Somalia, Bahrain finally forced the Obama regime to acknowledge that the Israeli 'model' of war, occupation and colonial rule via puppet regimes was not viable. The *reality principle* finally penetrated even the densest fog surrounding imperial advisers and strategists: the US empire was in retreat, Obama-Clinton were *not* custodians of an expanding empire, but rather the masters of imperial defeats. The empire-building project of the post-Cold War period, premised on unilateral action and military supremacy launched by Bush senior, continued by Clinton, expanded by Bush junior and multiplied by Obama, was a total and unmitigated failure by any imperial standards: prolonged losing wars were accompanied by a vast wave of pro-democracy uprisings, dumping prized imperial clients.

Colonial wars depleted the imperial treasury, impoverished citizens and undermined the "will to sacrifice" for the chimera of Global Greatness. The national mood was deeply disturbed by the cost of empire but also by the loss of global markets to new Asian competitors in China, India and elsewhere. Nowhere was the decline of the US more evident than in Latin America where new nationalist *reform* and developmental regimes secured divergent policies on key foreign policy issues, generated high growth, collaborated with new trading partners, decisively rejected several US-backed coups and repudiated Geithner's recycled free market dogma. There was *nowhere in the world* where the Obama regime could claim military victory, economic success or greater political influence.

As the reality of the deficits, losses and discontent entered the consciousness of key policymakers, a new imperial policy agenda took shape, not fully elaborated but improvised as circumstances dictated.

The Making of the "Obama Doctrine"

The first and foremost "recognition of reality" among the Obamites was that in a world of sovereign states, colonial land wars based on territorial armies of occupation were not viable. They led to prolonged resistance, extended budget over runs, continuing casualties and were definitely not "self-financing" as the Zionist geniuses in the Pentagon had once claimed. New forms of imperial warfare were needed to sustain the empire and destroy adversaries.

The hard choice facing the Obama regime with regard to Iraq was whether to admit defeat and retreat (in the sense that the US *cannot* retain a colonial presence and will leave behind an unreliable military and political configuration *expanding ties with Iran* and hostile to Israel), or to claim "victory´ in the sense of overthrowing Saddam Hussein and weakening Iraq's role in the Middle East. The retreat and defeat reality is now rationalized as a "repositioning" of 20,000 troops in the tiny city states run by despotic Gulf monarchies and the posting of war vessels in the Persian Gulf. Obama-Clinton claim the troops, war ships and aircraft carriers would re-enter Iraq if the current regime falls and a new nationalist movement comes to power. This is a doubtful proposition—as any "re-entry" would return the US to a prolonged, costly war. The main purpose of the repositioning is to protect the Gulf client dictatorships from their internal pro-democracy movements and to prepare to launch a joint US-Israeli air and sea attack on Iran. In other words troop retrenchment (as an occupying colonial power) is replaced by a build-up and concentration of air and sea power for attack and destruction of military and economic bases of the Iranian state.

The US retreat is a product of *defeat*; it is a *departure under duress*. The relocation of troops to petrol-despot mini-states is a downsizing of the US presence and a move to prop-up highly vulnerable corrupt clan based despots. The shift from Iraq to the Gulf States is a move to small, safe sanctuaries from a highly volatile conflictual major state with a history of resistance and independence. Since the US can no longer afford an unending large troop presence and cannot secure a 'residual force' its retreat to the Gulf States is making a virtue of necessity, a fall-back position to retain a launch pad for the next aerial war.

The Libyan war represents the key imperial formula for retaining Obama's imperial pretensions. The pretext for the war was just as phony as the *casus belli* in Iraq: in place of weapons of mass destruction, in Libya charges of genocide and rape were fabricated. A UN resolution claiming the right to militarily intervene to "protect civilians" was cooked up, and NATO launched an 8 month war consisting of nearly 30,000 air attacks to overthrow the established government and destroy the economy. Obama's Libyan policy was based on air and naval bombardment and Special Forces advisers; the use of a mercenary army and client ex-pats as the 'new leaders'; a multilaeral coalition of European empire builders (NATO) and Gulf state petrol-oligarchs. In contrast to Iraq and Afghanistan, sustained massive air attacks took the place of a large invasion army. Already Obama's military strategists have embraced and promulgated the Libyan experience as a new "Obama doctrine" for successfully rolling back independent Arab regimes and movements. Despite massive propaganda efforts to puff up the role of the mercenary 'rebels', the fact is that Gaddafi loyalists were only defeated by the combined air power of the NATO military command.

Obama-Clinton's celebration of the Libyan victory is *premature*: the means to victory involved the thorough destruction of the economy, from ports to irrigation systems to roads and hospitals, and the disarticulation of the labor force, with the forced flight of hundreds of thousands of sub-Sahara African workers and North African professionals. In other words it was a *pyrrhic* victory: Washington defeated an adversary; it has not *won* a viable state.

Even more serious, Washington's client mercenary ground forces include an amalgam of fundamentalist, tribal, gangster, and opportunist clan and neoliberal operators who have few interests in common. And all are armed and ready to carve up competing fiefdoms. The parallel is with Afghanistan where the US armed and financed drug traffickers, clan chiefs, warlords and fundamentalists to fight the secular pro-Soviet regime. Subsequent to destroying the regime, the same forces turned against the US and proceeded to spread a kind of pan-Islamic mobilization against pro-US client states and the US military presence throughout South-Central Asia, the Gulf States, the Middle East and North Africa. The US regards itself as using the Islamists, but the results demonstrate more clearly just exactly who was making better use of whom.

Obama's Libyan formula of using disparate mercenaries to achieve short term military success has boomeranged. Islamic fundamentalist militias and contrabandists are sending tons of ground-to-air missiles, machine guns and automatic rifles seized from Gaddafi's arms depots to Egypt, Syria, Somalia, Sudan and all points east, west, south and north. In a word, the volatile social and military conflicts among the new collaborator "rulers" in Libya has all the markings of a failed regime, in the context of which neither NATO nor oil companies can pretend to establish firm and secure bases of operation and exploitation.

The resort to missile warfare, especially the drone attacks on insurgents challenging US client regimes which figure so prominently in the "Obama doctrine," have succeeded in killing a few local commanders, but at a cost of alienating entire clans, villagers, townspeople and the general public in targeted countries. Drones' missiles are killing hundreds of civilians, causing relatives and ethnic kinspeople to join resistance groups. Up to the present, after 3 years of intensified "missile air warfare" the Obama regime has not secured a single major triumph over any of the targeted insurgencies by this means. The data available demonstrates the opposite. In Pakistan, not only has the entire northwest tribal area embraced the Islamic resistance but the vast majority of Pakistanis (80%) resent US drone violations of national sovereignty, forcing even otherwise docile officials to call into question their military ties with Washington. In Somalia and Yemen, drone and Special Forces' operations have had no impact in weakening the mass opposition to incumbent client regimes. Obama's long distance, high-tech warfare has been an ineffective substitute for large scale land wars.

The third dimension of the Obama doctrine, the heavy reliance on "third party" military intervention and/ or multilateral armed interventions, was not successful in Afghanistan and Iraq and was of limited effectiveness in Libya. The European multilateral forces retired early on in Iraq, unwilling to continue to spend on a war with no end and with virtually no support on the home front. The same process of short-term low level military multilateralism took place in Afghanistan: most NATO soldiers will be out *before* the US withdraws. The Libyan experience with "multilateral" air force collaboration in defeating Libya's armed forces destroyed the country, undermining any post-war reconstruction for decades. Moreover, "aerial multi-lateralism" followed the formula of "easy entry and fast exit"—leaving the mercenary predators in control on the ground. With their documented record of excelling in rape, pillage, torture and summary executions, only a brainless and morally depraved Hillary Clinton could sing the praises and dance a jig celebrating the victory of a knife wielding sodomist, torturing a captured President as "a victory for democracy".

The fourth dimension of the "Obama doctrine"— the use of foreign *mercenary armies*—has been tried and has failed in a number of cases where incumbent client rulers are under siege from resistance forces. The US financed the Ethiopian dictatorship's armed invasion of Somalia to prop up a corrupt, isolated regime holed up in the capital. After a prolonged futile effort to reverse the tide, the Ethiopian mercenary forces performed no better. They were then followed by the entry of the US backed Kenyan armed forces which has only led to massacres and starvation of hundreds of thousands of Somali refugees in Northern Kenya and Southern Somalia and deadly ambushes by the Islamic national resistance. These third party mercenary invasions have totally failed to secure the puppet regime; in fact they have aroused greater nationalist opposition. US backed "Third Party" mercenary armed interventions in Bahrain, where Saudi Arabian military forces put down a majoritarian uprising, has temporarily propped up the despotic monarchy but without dealing with the underlying demands of the pro-democracy mass movements.

The fifth dimension of the Obama doctrine is to use highly trained heavily armed "Special Forces" (SF) contingents of 500 more to assassinate insurgent leaders, to terrorize their rural supporters and to "give backbone" to the local military officials. Obama's October 2011 dispatch of a brigade of Special Forces to Uganda is a case in point. Up to now there are no reports of any decisive victories, even in this tiny country. The prospects for future use of this imperial tactic is probably limited to locales of limited geopolitical and economic significance with weak resistance movements—and only as a "complement" to local standing armies.

The final and probably most important element in the Obama doctrine is the promotion of civil-military mass uprisings and the reshuffle of elite figures to 'co-opt' popular pro-democracy movements in order to derail them from ending their country's' client relationship to Washington. Washington and the EU have incited and armed sectarian regional mass and armed movements aimed at overthrowing the authoritarian nationalist Assad regime in Syria. Playing off of legitimate democratic demands and harnessing fundamentalist hostility to a secular state, the US and EU, with the collaboration of Turkey and the Gulf states, have engaged in a triple policy of external sanctions, mass uprisings and armed resistance against the secular civilian majority and nationalist armed forces backing Basher Assad. Obama policy relies heavily on mass media propaganda and the exploitation of regional grievances to gain leverage for an eventual "regime change". But what kind of a regime will they get, at the end of it?

Parallel to the "outsider" political strategy in Syria, the Obama doctrine has adopted an insider strategy in Egypt and Tunisia. Faced with nationalist-pro-democracy social upheavals in Egypt, Washington financed and backed a military takeover and rule by an autocratic military junta which follows the basic foreign and domestic policies sustaining the economic structures under the Mubarak dictatorship. While cynically evoking the "spirit" of the Arab spring, Obama and Clinton, have backed the military tribunals which prosecute, torture and jail thousands of pro-democracy activists.

In the immediate period the Obama doctrine's use of 'external' and 'internal' civilian-military subversion has succeeded in derailing the promising anti-imperial movements that erupted in the early months of 2011. However, the great gulf that has opened between the recycled new client rulers and the pro-democracy movements has already led to calls for a 'second round' of uprisings to oust the opportunists "who have stolen the revolt" and betrayed the democratic principles of those who sacrificed to oust the client dictators. All the conditions which underlay the "Arab spring" are in place or have been exacerbated: unemployment, police repression, crony capitalism, inequalities and corruption. The experience of successful rebellion is still fresh and alive among the increasingly disenchanted youth. Like all of the new Obama imperial policies, the propping up of co-opted officials does not promise a reconsolidation of empire.

Conclusion: Wither the "Obama Doctrine"?

Consisting of reactive, improvised policies, with no overarching strategic framework, the so-called "Obama doctrine" shows few signs of reversing the decline of the US Empire. The deterioration of US "forward positions" in the Arab heartland is not linear nor without tactical advances, especially in light of the Obama regime's co-optation of several Islamic leaders in Libya, Syria and Tunisia and the temporary recycling of Mubarak era generals in Egypt.

Under cover of political euphemisms the Obama regime understates the scale and significance of its political and diplomatic losses: the forced withdrawal from Iraq is presented as a "successful mission in regime change", notwithstanding the burgeoning civil and regime violence between rival sectarian and secular factions (albeit achieving the Israeli objective of degrading and sowing anarchy in a strong Arab state—an achievement still largely in place). The US "withdrawal" from Afghanistan, is in reality a military retreat as the Taliban and related forces form a shadow government throughout the country and the huge mercenary army funded by billions of Pentagon dollar is infiltrated by Islamic-Nationalist militants.

The "drone attacks" presented as a successful new

counter-terror weapon crossing frontiers, is hyped as an effective cost-effective alternative to large scale ground invasions subject to prolonged armed resistance mainly provide sensational propaganda and public relations successes – having little impact revising the larger defeatist political reality.

On the diplomatic front US imperial decline is even more dramatic. The UN General Assembly votes against the US on Cuba, and the UNESCO vote on the admission of Palestine are overwhelmingly hostile to the Obama regime. Totally isolated, Washington's "retaliatory" posture of cutting off financial resources to UN-related bodies further reduces US institutional leverage.

As Obama submits to greater subservience to Israel's political arm in the US, the 52 Presidents of the Major American Jewish Organizations, and prepares a joint military attack on Iran, even NATO refuses to follow suit.

The great danger of the "Obama doctrine" is that it looks at short term 'local' consequences. Air and sea power can successfully bomb Iranian nuclear and military facilities, please the head of the Israeli ruling junta and guarantee American Zionist financial backing for Obama's re-election campaign. What is ignored is the military capacity of Iran to close the world's most important waterway (the Strait of Hormuz) shipping oil to Europe, Asia and the US. Obama's air war successes in Iran would be overwhelmed by Iranian ground and missile attacks of US forces throughout the Gulf. All US petrol allies in the region would be vulnerable to attack. Long range Iranian missiles would send millions of Israeli's scurrying for bomb shelters, even before Obama's Zionist advisers uncork their champagne to celebrate their "air victory" over Teheran. And in November 2011, Medvedev advised that Russia will aim its missiles at US-missile defense sites in Europe which, inter alia, presently protect Israel from Iranian retaliation...

The 'Obama doctrine' of extra-territorial air wars with impunity, if turned against Iran, would provoke a catastrophic conflagration, which would far surpass the disastrous outcome of the land wars in Iraq and Afghanistan. The "Obama doctrine" is in reality a set of improvised policies designed to deal with specific sets of circumstances based on a common overall problem: how to retain imperial domination in the face of failed colonial-occupation policies.

The tactical success in the air war against Libya and the opportunities opened by a Muslim-led uprising in Syria has given rise to the need to formulate a new overall strategy. Local collaborators are central, especially those with an institutional power base (such as the Egyptian military) or with levers of regional influence in civil society (Islamic movements in Syria—though surely the Afghan and Libyan precedents, in different ways, should be giving pause).

The attempt to generalize these 'tactical' gains into a general offensive strategy, however, founders on the fallacy of "misplaced concreteness". Iran is not Libya: it has the military power, geographic proximity and economic resources to demolish the weak and vulnerable 'peripheral' US client states. Israel can start a US war against the Islamic world—but it cannot win it. Netanyahu's losses in the UN cannot be explained away as 193 "anti-semitic" countries. The Zionist-US-Israeli troika are mutually masturbating in a closet. They can rant and rave and even precipitate an apocalyptic war, but Obama and Netanyahu are increasingly on the margin of significant world changes. Their policies are impotent reactions to popular movements envisioning historical transformations, which have even begun to enter into the center of empires: Wall Street and Tel Aviv. Ultimately the "Obama doctrine" is doomed to failure as it is incapable of recognizing that the problem of decline is not simply a problem of 'tactics' but a basic systemic breakdown of empire building—and the cracks and fissures abroad have ignited revolts at home.

WHAT FUTURE FOR THE WASHINGTON / "MODERATE ISLAM" ALLIANCE?

The dynamic of democratic, nationalist and class struggles throughout the Muslim world has set in motion a new constellation of alliances between the imperial West (US and European Union) and Islamist parties, leaders and regimes dubbed "moderate" by US officials, propagandists and academics.

This chapter analyzes the changing contemporary context of imperial domination, especially the demise of longstanding client regimes. It then examines the previous significant ties between western imperial powers and Islamist movements and regimes, and the basis of 'historical collaboration'.

We will outline the political circumstances in which the imperial powers seek to embrace these "moderate" Islamists who are now or will soon be in government as well as their historical and ongoing efforts to utilize "armed fundamentalists" in opposition to secular regimes. We will critically analyze how "moderate" Islam is defined by the Western imperialist powers. Is this a tactical alliance of last resort, born of necessity, to be swiftly changed by other better or more reliable partners once the opportunity presents, or is it a strategic alliance based on an inherent convergences of interests? What are the political "trade-offs"? What do imperialism's traditional neoliberal clients and their new 'moderate' Muslim allies have in common and how do they differ?

In conclusion we will evaluate the viability of these alliances and their capacity to contain and deflect the popular democratic movements and repress the burgeoning class and national struggles, especially in regard to the 'obstacles' posed by the Israel-US-Zionist ties and the continued IMF policies which promise to worsen the crises in the Muslim countries.

The Transition from Neoliberal Client Rulers to Power-Sharing with Moderate Islamists

It should be noted that throughout the region, during the period of secular client regimes, the primary opposition was Islamist. With leaderships driven into exile, and supporters imprisoned or slaughtered, these groups through the protection of the mosque, tolerated by the ruling dictatorships, gained a popular following, their history of charity and welfare programs giving them what more recent comers to the struggle view as an unfair advantage. The key motivation in the turn by Washington and the European imperial troika (England, France and Germany) to the "moderate Islamists" was the collapse or weakening of their long-term client rulers. Faced with the ouster of Mubarak, in Egypt, Ali in Tunisia and Saleh in Yemen as well as mass protests in Morocco and Algeria, the US-EU first attempted to promote neoliberal-military coalitions .

However, as subsequent elections made clear, these groups enjoyed neither the longstanding grassroots political organization nor the popular appeal of the traditional Islamic opposition. Western imperialists turned to conservative Muslim leaders who were willing to work within the existing state institutional framework by participating in elections rather than attempting to combat the NATO and Israel-backed ruling military junta by joining the ongoing popular demonstrations in the street. In Egypt, the Freedom and Justice Party (FJP) (the political arm of the Muslim Brotherhood), in Tunisia the Renaissance Party, in Morocco the Justice and Development Party have all *blocked* the pro-democracy street movements that challenge the socio-economic status quo and the long-standing military-imperial linkages so that elections could go forward.

The Islamists are called "moderate and respectable" because they agreed to participate in elections *within the boundaries of the established political and economic order*. As at this writing (after the first of three rounds of elections in Egypt), they have dropped any criticism of imperial and colonial treaties and trade agreements signed by the previous client regimes—including those which collaborate with Israel's colonization of Palestine.

Equally important, "moderate" means *supporting imperial wars* against nationalist and secular Arab republics, such as Syria and Libya, and isolating and/or repressing class based trade unions and secular-left parties—though the Nasserist Karama Party is a part of the Egyptian Muslim Brotherhood's election coalition, the Democratic Alliance.

"Moderate" Islamists will be forced to become the Empire's 'contraceptive of choice' against any chance the massive Arab peoples' revolt might give birth to substantive egalitarian social changes and bring those brutal pro-western officials, responsible for so many crimes against humanity, to justice.

Now, for want of viable liberal, secular alternatives, the West and their client officials in the military and police have agreed to a kind of "power-sharing' (i.e. they are allowing the elections to take place) with those they deem the moderate/respectable (read 'reactionary') Islamist parties, with a view to ensuring that post elections affairs might shape up as follows: The Islamists would be responsible for imposing orthodox economic policies and re-establishing 'order' (i.e. bolstering the existing one) in partnership with pro-multinational bank economists and pro US-EU generals and security officials. In exchange the Islamists could take certain ministries, appoint their members, finance electoral clientele among the poor and push their 'moderate' religious, social and cultural agenda. Basically, the elected Islamists would replace the old corrupt dictatorial regimes in running the state and signing off on more free trade agreements with the EU. Their role would be to keep the leftists, nationalists and populists out of power and from gaining mass support. Their job would be to substitute spiritual solace and "inner worth" via Islam in place of redistributing land, income and power from the elite, including the foreign multinationals to the peasants, workers, unemployed and exploited low-paid employees.

Why the Empire Arms Fundamentalist Anti-Secular Muslims

While the US and EU have backed respectable "moderate Islam" in heading off a popular upheaval of the young and unemployed, in other contexts they have enlisted violent, fundamentalist Islamic terrorists to overthrow secular independent anti-imperialists regimes—like Libya, Syria—just as they had done earlier in Afghanistan and Yugoslavia. The US, Qatar and the European troika financed and armed Libyan fundamentalist militias and then engaged in a murderous eight months air and sea assault to ensure their client's 'victory' over the secular Gaddafi regime. Fresh from NATO's success, the US, the European 'Troika' and Turkey, with the backing of the League of Arab collaborator princes and emirs, have financed a violent Muslim Brotherhood insurrection in Syria, intent on destroying the heavily public sector economy and modern secular state.

The US and EU have openly unleashed their fundamentalists allies in order to destroy independent adversaries in the name of "democracy" and 'humanitarian intervention', a laughable claim in light of decade long colonial wars of occupation in Iraq and Afghanistan. All

114

targeted regimes have one crime in common: Using their national resources to develop states independent of imperial dictates.

NATO implements its campaigns through conservative 'moderate' or armed fundamentalist Islamist movements depending on the specific needs, circumstances and range of options in any given target nation. With the fall of pro-Empire 'secular dictatorships' in Egypt and Tunisia, pliable conservative Islamist leaders are the fall back "lesser evil".

On the other hand, when the opportunity to overthrow an independent secular or nationalist regime arises, armed and violent fundamentalist mercenaries become the imperialists' political vehicle of choice. As with European empires in the past, the modern Western imperial countries have relied on retrograde religious parties and leaders to collaborate and serve their economic and military interests and to provide mercenaries for imperial armies to savage any anti-imperialist secular revolutionaries. In that sense US and European rulers are neither 'pro nor anti' Islam, it all depends on their *national and class position*. Islamists who collaborate with Empire are "moderate" allies and if they attack an anti-imperialist regime, they become 'freedom fighters'. On the other hand, they become "terrorists" or "fundamentalists" when they oppose imperial occupation, pillage or colonial settlements.

Contemporary History of Islamist-Imperial Collaboration

The historical record of western imperial expansion reveals many instances of collaboration and cooptation as well as conflict with Islamist regimes, movements and parties. In the early 1960s the CIA backed a brutal military coup against the secular Indonesian nationalist regime of Sukarno, and encouraged their puppet dictator General Suharto to unleash Muslim militia in a veritable "holy war" exterminating nearly one million leftist trade unionists, school teachers, students, farmers, communists or suspected sympathizers and their family members. The horrific 'Jakarta Option' became a model for CIA operations elsewhere. In Yugoslavia the US and Europe promoted and financed fundamentalist Muslims in Bosnia, importing mujahedeen who came to aid them, and would later form part of Al Qaeda, and then backed the Kosovo Liberation Army, a known terrorist (ethnically Muslim but not Islamist) organization, in order to completely break up and ethnically 'cleanse' a modern secular multinational state—leading to Americans and NATO bombing Belgrade for the first time since the Nazis in the Second World War.

During President Carter's administration, at the instigation of Brzezinski and Bernard Lewis, the CIA joined with Saudi Arabia's ruling royalty in providing billions of dollars in arms and military supplies to Afghan Muslim fundamentalists in their brutal but successful Jihad overthrowing a modern, secular nationalist regime backed by the USSR. The murderous fate of school teachers and educated women in the aftermath was quickly covered up.

Needless to say, wherever US imperialism faces leftist or secular, modernizing *anti-imperialist* regimes, Washington turns to retrograde Islamic leaders willing and able to destroy the progressive regime in return for imperialist support. Such coalitions are built mainly around fundamentalist and moderate Islamist opposition to class-based politics allied with the Empire's hostility to any anti-imperialist challenge to its domination.

The same 'coalition' of Islamists and the Empire has been glaringly obvious during the NATO assault on Libya and continues against Syria. The Muslims provide the shock troops on the ground; NATO provides the aerial bombing, funds, arms, sanctions, embargoes and propaganda.

These Islamist-Imperialist coalitions are usually temporary, based on a common secular or nationalist enemy and not on any common strategic interest. After the defeat of a secular anti-imperialist regime, militant Muslims may then find themselves attacked by the colonial neoliberal regime most favored by the imperial west. This happened in Afghanistan and elsewhere after the overseas Islamist fighters (Afghan Arabs) returned to their own neo-colonized, collaborating home countries, like Saudi Arabia, Algeria and Egypt and elsewhere.

Contemporary History of Islamist-Imperial Conflict

The relation between Islamist regimes and imperialism is complex, changing and full of examples of bloody conflict.

The US backed the "modernizing" free market dictatorship of the Shah in Iran, overthrowing the nationalist Mosaddegh regime. They provided arms and intelligence for the Savak, the Shah's monstrous secret police as it hunted down and murdered tens of thousands of nationalist-Islamists and leftist resistance fighters and critics in Iran and abroad. The rise to power of the fundamentalist-anti-imperialist Khomeini regime fueled US armed attacks and provoked retaliatory moves: Iran backed and financed anti-colonial Islamist groups in Lebanon (Hezbollah), Palestine (Hamas) and Iraq (the Shia parties).

Subsequent to 9/11 the US invaded and overthrew the Islamist Taliban regime and re-colonized the country, establishing a puppet regime under US-European auspices. The Taliban and allied Islamist and nationalist resistance fighters organized and established a mass guerrilla army which has engaged in a decade long war with armed support from Pakistani Islamist forces responding to US military incursions.

In Palestine, Washington, under the overweening control of Israel's Zionist fifth column, has armed and financed Israel's war against the popularly elected Palestinian Islamist Hamas government in Gaza. Washington's total commitment to the Jewish state and its colonial expansion and usurpation of Palestinian (Muslim and Christian) lands and property in Jerusalem and elsewhere reflects the profound and pervasive *influence* of the Zionist power configuration throughout the US political system. It regularly secures 90% votes in Congress, pledges of allegiance from the White House, and senior appointments in Treasury, State Department and the Pentagon.

What determines whether the US Empire will have a collaborative or conflict-ridden relation with Islam depends on the specific political context. The US allies with Islamists when faced with nationalist, leftist and secular democratic regimes and movements, especially where their optimal choice, a military-neoliberal alternative is relatively weak. However, faced with a nationalist, anti-colonial Islamist regime (as is the case of the Islamic Republic of Iran), Washington will side with pro-western liberals, dissident Muslim clerics, pliable tribal chiefs, separatist ethnic minorities and pro-Western generals.

The key to US-Islamist relations from the White House perspective is based on the Islamists' attitude toward empire, class politics, NATO and the "free market" (private foreign investment).

To the extent that today's 'moderate' Islamist parties in Tunisia, Egypt, Turkey, Morocco (and elsewhere), which have offered their support to NATO and its wars against Libya and Syria, seek to uphold 'private property' (i.e. foreign and imperialist client control of key industries) and repress independent working class and anti-imperialist parties, they are effectively the Empire's "new partners" in the pillage of the resource-rich Middle East and North Africa. Not until they actually renounce and seek to throw off the treaties, agreements, dependencies and financial architecture of global neoliberalism, can they claim to be otherwise.

The US-brokered counter-revolutionary alliance among moderate Islamists, the previous military rulers and Washington is fraught with tensions. The military demands total impunity and a continuation of its economic privileges; this includes a veto on any legislation addressing the previous regime's brutal crimes against its own people. On the other hand, the Islamist parties uphold their electoral victories and demand majority rule. Washington insists the alliance adhere to its policy toward Israel and abandon their support for the Palestinian national struggle. As these tensions and conflicts deepen, the alliance could collapse ushering in a new phase of conflict and instability.

Emblematic of "moderate Islamiist" collaboration with US-EU imperialism is the role of Qatar, home to the 'respectable' Arabic media giant, Al-Jazeera, and the demagogic Qatari "spiritual guide" Sheik Youssef al-Qaradawi. Sheik Youssef quotes the Qur'an and Islamic moral principles in defense of NATO's 8-month aerial bombing of Libya, which killed over 50,000 pro-regime Libyans (themselves Muslims). He called for armed imperial intervention in Syria to overthrow the secular Assad regime, a position he shares comfortably with the state of Israel. He urged the "moderate Islamists" in Egypt and Tunisia to cease any criticism of the existing economic order.[1] In a word, this respectable Muslim cleric seems to be NATO's perfect Qur'an-quoting "moderate Islamist" partner—a dream come true—and accordingly, he is puffed by the *Financial Times*.[2]

The Strategic Utility of "Moderate" Islamist Parties

Islamist parties are approached by the Empire's policy elites only when they have a mass following and can therefore weaken any popular, nationalist insurgency. Mass-based Islamist parties serve the empire by providing "legitimacy", by winning elections and by giving a veneer of respectability to the pro-imperial military and police apparatus retained in place from the overthrown client state dictatorships.

The Islamist parties compete at the "grass roots" with the leftists. They build up a clientele of supporters among the poor in the countryside and urban slums through organized charity and basic social services administered at the mosques and humanitarian religious foundations. Because they reject class struggle and are intensely hostile to the left (with its secular, pro-feminist and working-class agenda), they have been 'half-tolerated' by the dictatorship insofar as their activities provide a social support network, hence blunting popular desperation, while the leftist activists, engaged specifically in political protest, are routinely murdered. Subsequently, with the overthrow of the dictatorship, the Islamists' base emerges intact with the strongest national organizational network as the country's 'natural leaders' from the religious-bazaar merchant political elite. Their leaders, if they remain focused on morality, culture, religion and households (women), in other words, the "micro-society, will end up serving the empire and its traditional native military collaborators in exchange for a 'slice of power'.

In turn, they effectively marginalize and undermine the left, anti-imperialist secular democrats in the streets. In the face of mass popular rebellion calling into question the imperial order, a 'moderate' Islamist-imperial partnership is a 'heavenly deal' praised in Washington, Paris or London (as well as Riyadh and Tel Aviv).

Conclusion: How Viable is the Imperial-Islamic Coalition?

Those who thought that the spontaneous pro-democracy movements spelled the end of the imperial order left out the role of organized "moderate" Islamist electoral parties as able collaborators of Empire. The brutally repressed mass mobilization of unemployed youth was no match for the well-funded grass roots community organization of the moderate Islamists. This is especially true when politics shifted from the street to the ballot box, a process that the Islamist parties facilitated. In the absence of a mass revolutionary party able to seek state power by revolutionary means, the existing military-police state was able to work around the mass protesters and put together a power sharing agreement—at least in the short-run.

In the November 2011 elections, the radical Egyptian Islamist party, *Nour,* gathered one-quarter of the vote in Cairo and Alexandria. Their showing was even higher among the urban poor districts, which promises even greater support among poor rural constituencies in the coming elections. Essentially a Salafist Islamist party, *Nour,* unlike the Muslim Brotherhood, combined denunciations of class abuses and elite corruption with mass appeals to a return to a mythic harmonious life. They used effective grass roots organizing around basic services in order to gain a greater proportion of the working class vote than all the leftist parties combined. *Nour's* message of "class retribution against the ...abuses of Egypt's elite fueled *Nour's* new found popularity".[3]

Despite the (mixed) successes of the Islamist-Imperial partnership—the defeat of the Soviets in Afghanistan, the increasingly fractious cooperation of Turkey (now at outs with Israel), regime change in Libya, and possibly Syria— the world economic crises and especially the growing unemployment and misery in the Arab countries will make it difficult for the 'respectable moderate' Islamists to stabilize their societies. The 'orthodox neoliberal framework' imposed by the Empire will constrain them from addressing the needs of the popular masses. The "moderate" Islamists will try to co-opt some secular liberals, social democrats and even a few leftists as 'minority partners' to share the responsibility for dashing the expectations of the poor in their countries.

The fact of the matter is that the pro-imperial Islamist parties have absolutely no answer to the current crises. While charities and social services delivered from the mosque in the communities during the dictatorship won them mass support, if they now impose more austerity programs from their ministerial posts, it will certainly alienate and infuriate their mass base. What will follow depends on who is best organized: Liberals are limited to media campaigns and tied to economic orthodoxy; the leftists would have to advance from protest movements in the downtown squares to organized political units operating in popular neighborhoods, workplaces, markets, villages and slums. Otherwise radical fundamentalist, like the Salafists,

121

will exploit the people's outrage with moderate Islamist betrayals and promote their own version of a closed clerical society, opposing the West while repressing the Left.

The US and EU may have 'temporarily' avoided revolution by accommodating electoral reforms and adapting to alliances with "moderate" Islamists, but their ongoing military interventions and their own growing economic crisis will *simply postpone* a more decisive conflict in the near future.

ENDNOTES

1   See "Spiritual guide steers Arabs to moderation", *Financial Times*, December 9, 2011, p. 5.

2   But it was only in 2008 that he was denied entry to the United Kingdom on the grounds of his defense of Palestinian suicide attacks on Israelis as "martyrdom in the name of God", during a BBC interview. In fact his support of the Palestinian struggle has been expressed by numerous fatwas. Is it reasonable to presume that such a figure will be on board for the entire Western imperialist package, a primary component of which is peace, if not complicity with Israeli occupation of Palestine?

3   *Financial Times*, December 10, 2011 p. 6.

INDICATORS OF SOCIAL WELL BEING IN LIBYA

**Trends in Libyan Arab Jamahiriya's
Human Development Index (HDI) 2005-2010**

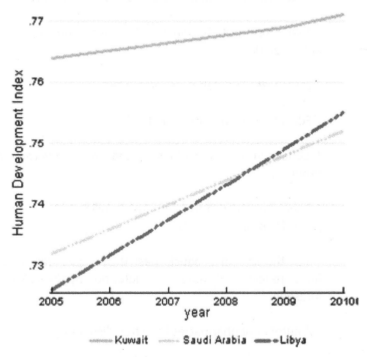

The Libyan Arab Jamahiriya's 2010 HDI of 0.755 is above the average of 0.593 for countries in the Arab States. It is also above the average of 0.717 for high human development countries.
Source: <http://hdrstats.undp.org/images/explanations/LBY.pdf

The following are only a few of the indicators of social well-being[1] that speak to the efforts of the Gaddafi government to improve the lot of the Libyan people:

* Libya's GDP per capita is $ 14,192.

* For each family member the state pays a $ 1,000 yearly subsidy.

* Unemployed are paid 730 $ monthly.

* The salary of a hospital nurse is $ 1,000.

* For every newborn $ 7,000 is paid .

* Newly weds are donated $ 64,000 to buy an apartment.

* To open a private business one gets a one-time financial aid of $20 000 .

* Large taxes and duties are prohibited.

* Education and medicine are free.

* Education and Internships abroad are at government expense.

* There are chain stores for large families with symbolic prices for basic foodstuffs.

* For the sale of products past their expiry date large fines are levied, in some cases detention by the police is foreseen.

* A number of pharmacies have free dispensing.

* Counterfeiting medication is considered a major crime.

* No rental payments.

* No payment for electricity for the population.

* The sale and use of alcohol is prohibited, "prohibition" is a law.

* Loans for buying a car and an apartment are given at no interest.

* Real estate services are prohibited.

* If an individual decides to buy a car up to 50% of the price is paid by the state, to militia guards it donates 65% of the price.

* Gasoline is cheaper than water. A liter of gasoline costs $ 0.14.[2] The profits from oil sale were spent on the population welfare and rising life standards.

* In Libya, much money is spent on irrigation by the country's groundwater, the amount of which is about 100 annual runoffs of the Nile. By its scale, this water project has earned itself the name of "the Eighth Wonder of the World." It provides 5-million cubic meters of water a day across the desert, greatly increasing the irrigated area. 4,000 kilometers of pipes are buried deep into the ground to secure them from the heat. All that was needed for the project was carried out mostly by Libya herself. Nothing was bought in the First World... With this water project, Libya was able to start a real "green revolution", in the literal sense, that would solve a lot of problems with food in Africa. And most importantly, it would ensure stability and economic independence. At one time, Gaddafi said that Libya's water project would be "the strongest response to America, which accuses Libya of supporting terrorism." [3]

The high standing of Libya in the UN's Human Development Index is due to its natural wealth being used, not only to promote the well being of Libyans, but also to promote development and advancement in the African continent itself.

Libya holds oil reserves of an estimated 60 billion barrels, especially valuable due to their low extraction costs, as well as a further estimated 1,500 billion cubic metres in natural gas reserves. Once the embargo against Libya was lifted in 2004, Libya was able to maintain a trade surplus of $30 billion (which Gaddafi proposed should be disbursed directly to the Libyan people). The Libyan Investment Authority (LIA) manages sovereign wealth funds of a value of approxiamtely $70 billion, to say nothing of Central Bank reserves, estimated at $150 billion, possibly more—now frozen by the US and the EU.[4]

In addition to investments in over 25 African countries, 22 of which were in sub-Saharan Africa, Libya invested in the implementation of three financial institutions in Africa, the African Investment Bank, based in Tripoli, the African Monetary Fund, based in Yaoundé (Cameroon), the African Central Bank, with Based in Abuja (Nigeria).

The development of these bodies would enable African countries to escape the control of the World Bank and International Monetary Fund, tools of neo-colonial domination, and would mark the end of the CFA franc, the currency that 14 former French colonies are forced to use. Freezing Libyan funds deals a strong blow to the entire project.[5]

Libya is one of the few remaining countries in the world to entirely own its Central Bank. It is highly noteworthy that the Libyan "rebels", however disorganized and scattered they may have been militarily, appear to have been sufficiently attuned to high finance to have swiftly announced the "[d]esignation of the Central Bank of Benghazi as a monetary authority competent in monetary policies in Libya and appointment of a Governor to the Central Bank of Libya, with a temporary headquarters in Benghazi." along with the creation of a new Libyan Oil Company.[6]

ENDNOTES

1   Helen Shelestiuk, Libya: Facts and Analysis < http://left.ru/2011/2/shelestiuk204.phtml>

2   <http://www.echosevera.ru/politics/2011/03/17/314.html> cited in Shelestuk, id.

3   Ye Kholmogorov, Gaddafi: questions, answers and lessons of history <http://www.imperiya.by/rusworld.html?id=9379> cited in Shelestuk, id.

4   Manlio Dinucci, "Financial Heist of the Century: Confiscating Libya's Sovereign Wealth Funds (SWF)", *Il Manifesto* (translated from Italian), 04-22-2011, sourced at <http://www.globalresearch.ca/index.php?context=va&aid=24479>

5   Id.

6   Alex Newman, "'Libyan Rebels' Create Central Bank, Oil Company", www.globalresearch.ca, April 14, 2011, at <http://www.globalresearch.ca/index.php?context=viewArticle&code=NEW20110413&articleId=24308>

INDEX

A

Africa 11-13, 48, 51-53, 57, 58, 61, 66-
68, 70, 75, 78, 79, 82, 85, 94, 124, 125
North Africa 19,26, 41,
43, 74, 87, 91, 103, 118 African mercenary
forces 49 African migrant workers 77-
78, 103
African Union 83-85
AFRICOM 12, 13, 46, 53, 70
Aid 34, 60, 65, 85 military aid 25, 26, 34
USAID 34
AIPAC 17
Al Jazeera 119
Al Qaeda 45, 48, 49, 78, 88-90, 93, 95, 96
Al Qaeda in the Arabian Peninsula 94 Al
Qaeda in Iraq 89
Al-Assad, Bashar 82, 84, 106
Al-Awlaki, Anwar 93-98
Algeria 17, 52, 67, 80, 112, 117
Al-Zawahiri, Dr. Ayman 87
Arms industry 28, 32, 52
Assassination 58, 78, 87-92, 93-98

B

Bahrain 29, 39, 50, 79, 80-82, 95, 97, 101,
106
Banks 30, 57, 68, 78, 82, 83; Libyan central
bank 57, 126
Ben Ali, Zin El Abidine 80, 101
Benghazi 46, 47, 55, 76, 126
Bin Laden, Osama 87-94
Black Libyans 48, 58, 77, 78, 85
Brazil 16, 42, 52, 71
Bush Administration 20, 44, 45, 49, 99,
100
Bush, George Herbert Walker 11, 101
Bush, George Walker 12, 101

C

Cameron, David 54
Chile 16, 66, 86
China 39, 42, 44, 52, 61, 67, 69-72, 103,
CIA 23-28, 47, 53, 54, 58, 73, 93-95, 115,
116
Civil society 13, 21, 79, 80, 110
Civil war 19, 21, 49, 50, 54, 55, 82
Class 29, 30, 34, 38, 115, 121; middle 22,
29, 31, 34, 35, 64, 86; working 21, 35,
86, 118, 119, 121; rentier 30-39; ruling
30, 31, 32, 34, 62, 72, 84, 85; Class
struggle 36, 111, 112, 118, 119
Clinton, Bill 11, 12
Clinton, Hillary 74, 101, 102, 106, 107
Collaborators 13, 18, 26, 28, 47, 60, 62,
66, 89, 91, 92, 96, 99-101, 104, 110,
114, 120-122,
Colonialism 12, 26, 28, 32, 39, 56, 60, 70,
71, 76, 77-80, 83-86, 90, 99, 101-103,
110, 113-118, 126
Congo 11, 12
Congress 12, 19-21, 27, 39
Cuba 16, 17, 109

D

Democrats 100
Democracy 13, 61, 63, 74, 80, 83, 85, 107,
108, 111-113, 118, 120
Development 30, 33, 35, 38, 61, 66, 72,
85, 102, 123, 125
Dictators 13, 15-17, 20-26, 28, 29, 32, 41,
47, 80, 94, 115
Djibouti 11,
Drone warfare 81, 93, 95, 105, 108

E

Egypt 9, 11, 13, 15, 17, 18, 20, 21, 23-29,
33-35, 37, 49, 51, 67, 71, 79, 80, 81, 84,